ALS Saved My Life
until it didn't

Dr. Jenni Kleinman Berebitsky
with Joyce Kleinman & Elizabeth Flynn

Front cover original artwork by Hildy Eppel Hassman
Cover design and interior photo composition by Joyce Kleinman
Inside book design by Tim Gaskins

Library of Congress Cataloging-in-Publication Data
Berebitsky, Jenni
ALS Saved My Life… *until it didn't*: Jenni Berebitsky/Memoir
p. cm.
ISBN 978-0-692-06669-0
1. Jenni Berebitsky 2. Memoir I. Title
Original Printing 2018

In Praise of *ALS Saved My Life. . . until it didn't*

When Jenni says in this book that she had to get weak to find her strength, you better believe it. She's one of the strongest people I have ever met, and this book of hers is mighty indeed. It will make you laugh, make you cry, and make you see the wonder and beauty of life. Read it now, and you'll share some of Jenni's strength.

> —Jonathan Eig, New York Times best-selling author of
> *Luckiest Man: The Life and Death of Lou Gehrig*

An honest and sobering glimpse into our daily struggles, of first being diagnosed, and then living with ALS. Jenni fights forward with grace, demonstrating that even under these difficult and painful circumstances; being present in the moment and making space for joy, humor, and love, opens the door for meaning, and gratitude in each and every day. Jenni you inspire me!

> —Nanci Ryder, Hollywood publicist, Co-founder of
> BWR Public Relations, diagnosed with ALS in 2014

Beautifully done - I would of given anything to have read a book like this to prepare ourselves . . . you are going to help and inspire so many people. AMAZING - THANK YOU both for coming into our lives.

> —Kathy Shawver Maffei, close friend of Nanci Ryder for
> over 20 years

For a story of terminal illness, this book is overflowing with joy, optimism, good humor, and the love of life. Every page reminds us of how fragile our lives are, but also of Abraham Lincoln's maxim that "most folks are about as happy as they make up their minds to be." Jenni Berebitsky has made her mind up to be happy, and to be strong, and to lend her happiness and strength to the people around her—including those lucky enough to read this courageous memoir.

—Ben H. Winters, Author of nine novels, including most recently the New York Times bestselling *Underground Airlines*

We are all just one bad diagnosis from stepping into the unknown territory that Jenni and her family have traveled. Like pioneers, they've blazed a trail for those who follow and they've done it with humor and pragmatism.

     —Mary Doria Russell, Author of *The Sparrow, A Thread of Grace,* and *Doc*

As Jenni says, "I'm always thinking," which the reader sees clearly in her creativity and ways of connecting to the world around her. She is not helpless. At varying points in her disease progression, she opens her own naturopathic medical practice, officiates at her brother's wedding, and participates in a sprint triathlon—twice. And throughout the entire story, Jenni shows us what a difference a wry sense of humor can make, especially when we are in our most vulnerable states. Jenni Berebitsky's memoir has the reader reconsider the idea of what it means to be healthy and fully alive. She reminds us that "angels can appear out of nowhere," and that if we are paying attention, and if we are always thinking, we just might see them.

     —Melissa Keller, author of *Crazy is Relative*

This book is incredible. So raw and real -- and inspiring. It puts life into perspective in a way you've probably never seen. It brings joy, anger, tears and laughter. I soaked in every single word.

     —Dana Benbow, Indianapolis Star writer

Table of Contents

Dedication

I dedicate this book to all those struggling with life-altering challenges. Each of you has your own story to tell. I hope that my account of my life will resonate with you and speak to you.

Helping Hands Blanket

A composite of Jenni's Villagers' personal interpretation of their Helping Hands, printed on a fleece blanket for Jenni for her 40th birthday.

Acknowledgments

With all my heart, I want to thank my husband, Jeff Berebitsky, and my mom, Joyce Kleinman. Without you I would not be who I am or where I am. You have helped me mentally, physically, emotionally, and spiritually. Many have been my arms and legs, but the two of you have carried me through.

Jeff and I joke that ALS is not for sissies. Jeff, you are no sissy! I wonder if any of us notices the fine print of our wedding vows. Not only did you read them, but also you took them seriously. That is who you are. You are a man of integrity and honor. Your courage and patience are unparalleled. Thank you for being my husband, my love, and my friend.

Some say you can't judge a book by its cover, but in this case, I hope you do. Thank you Hildy Eppel Hassman for bringing life to my abstract thoughts and clipart, and making my vision into this beautiful watercolor painting.

A sincere thank you to Elizabeth Flynn who helped me get started on this book. I had a growing need to tell my story, but I didn't know where to begin. Elizabeth, without your interviewing skills, guiding questions, and organizing expertise, this book never would have happened.

Where Elizabeth left off, others stepped in. First, I want to thank Joyce, my mom, for being my fingers, my co-conspirator, and sometimes my brain. We spent countless hours together. She typed on her iPad and projected it on to the TV as I transformed my stories, experiences, and lessons learned into words worthy of your time. My mom then became my manager/publisher/designer and all around right-hand. She was committed that my dream become a reality. A new quote: "Behind every successful woman is a persistent mom."

Next, thank you to all who read, reviewed, edited, and helped in various ways as the book took shape: Beth Peyton, Beverly Zisla Welber, Carolyn McConkey, Christine Melton, Debi Kleinman, Donna Dorman, Donna Krichiver, Heather Morrall, Hildy Eppel Hassman, Janice Lynch Schuster, Jeanne Beckwith, Judy Peres, Kara Faris, Kathi Cummings, Kylea Asher-Smith, Leslie Dinneen, Lisa Boncosky, Lyn O'Brien, Lynn Valinetz, Mark Steingold, Melissa Keller, Susan Youdovin, Tayla Lee, and Tessa Heady.

Together we completed the many steps it takes to write and publish a book.

To my amazing, kind, and generous family and friends—my helpers for the day, Jenni's Village, THANK YOU! You are all invaluable to me. I can't imagine what my life would be like without each and every one of you. It takes a Village to raise a Jenni.

And last but not least, Philip. This book is for you. You are my joy! You're the sweetest, most charismatic person I've ever met. I'm so proud that you are my son. You are a wonderful human being, a gift to many. Know that I will always love you and be there for you.

Joyce and Jenni's creative writing process.
Working on iPad, projecting on TV.

Philip, son; Joyce, mom; Jenni; Jeff, husband;
Gerri, sister-in-law; & Rob, brother
(8 years, 7 months after diagnosis)

2014 Indianapolis Sprint Triathlon
Jenni's Village Cheering Section

Preface

Thank you for picking up this book. In some ways, it takes courage to read. Parts might be funny; other parts sad; some moving; but mostly my goal is to help you understand what life is like with ALS—Amyotrophic Lateral Sclerosis, sometimes called Lou Gehrig's disease. Whether you have ALS, or someone you know and love does, or you just want to understand the disease, I hope you find insight into how to move forward after life-altering circumstances.

You may find that while reading this book, you sometimes think: "I'm not ready for that!"

That's okay. It's part of the process. Feel free to stop reading when you need to and then come back when you are ready. Or find a chapter that relates to your current situation.

You may be tempted to paint me as the hero, Jeff the martyr, and ALS the villain. Truth be told, I'm not a hero, but there is no question that ALS is a son of a bitch.

The title of this book started as a joke when I would say ALS was the best thing to happen to my nails and face. I used to be a picker, but now with non-functioning hands, my nails and face are the healthiest they have ever been. But the more I joked about this, the more I came to realize that in bizarre ways, ALS has made my life richer.

My experiences have taught me we don't know how we will handle something until it's right in front of us. We have two choices when faced with such uncertainty: give up or move forward. I've chosen to move forward and in the process, this disease has taught me humility, patience, and perseverance.

Despite being frequently kicked in the butt, I am able to pause and realize that things could always be worse. I take stock of my blessings. For instance, ALS has brought Jeff and me closer. I am so grateful for our communication and his unflappable love and support. We are also very fortunate that this disease has not crippled us financially as it does to so many. Over the course of the last eight years, we have had enormous support from family and friends. We call them "Jenni's Villagers."

Then there are the "perks": e.g., "Princess Parking," skipping past the lines at the airport and amusement parks, scoring amazing seats for *Hamilton the Musical* at a fraction of the cost, getting to see live tapings of *The Oprah Winfrey Show* twice and lots more. There is an *ALS Card*; I am a proud card-carrying member and not afraid to use it.

I'm often told that I have the patience of a saint. I'm able to be this way with people because I'm always thinking about what I would do if I were in their shoes. I admire the courage it takes to be with me. I realize that ALS not only affects me, but also everyone in my life.

Being with me causes others to step out of their comfort zone. They are often called on to do more than they thought they could—whether it is being more creative, resourceful, and patient, or emotionally and physically stronger. Perhaps, the hardest thing of all is the level of selflessness needed when caring for someone with limited abilities. The patient's needs often have to come before the caregiver's. I sometimes wonder if the situation were reversed, would I rise to the many challenges or fall short and screw something up?

To get a sense of what it's like for someone with ALS, I highly recommend you read *Walk a Mile in My Shoes or At Least Five Minutes* found in Appendix D.

My mind is fully functional, but my body continues to fail piece by piece. As my mom says, "Jenni runs her household and her life, but she just needs others to be her hands and feet." My community is always adjusting their way of doing things to try to accommodate my desires and my ever-changing needs. Basically, "I'm here to keep it interesting."

Jenni 7/13/13 (4 years, 4 months after diagnosis)

Foreword

by Elizabeth Flynn

Jenni was determined to write a book about her life with ALS and Barb, Jenni's mother-in-law and my next door neighbor, asked if I would help. Since I agreed, I was obviously going to have to meet Jenni. When that day came, I was apprehensive. How was this even going to work? Does ALS affect your mental capacity? Would she be able to handle a project like this?

I just didn't want to believe the possibility that someone so young could be stricken with ALS. An old classmate of my husband's recently died of ALS and it sounded like such a horrifying disease, I was frightened to even meet Jenni. Barb had told me about her and showed me the article in the newspaper about her heroic participation in the Indianapolis Sprint Triathlon the previous summer where she emerged as somewhat of a local celebrity.

The first time I came to meet Jenni at Barb's, I cautiously approached her wheelchair. I kept some distance between us and said hello to her rather loudly as if she had a hearing problem or something. She looked up at me and smiled the most dazzling smile, so wide it dimpled her cheeks, so bright sunbeams paled, and I was not only instantly at ease, I was spellbound.

The pretty 39-year-old looked healthy and vibrant, her skin sun-kissed and glowing, her blonde hair thick and shiny—all of which didn't jibe with a terminal diagnosis. In fact, for a moment I wondered how bad off could she be? ALS shouldn't look like this.

In a short time talking with her, I found that not only could she hear me but had all her wits about her and was as delightful as she was radiant. Again I was puzzled. Why is she so happy? How could she beam when at this point in her illness all she could do physically, other than move her head, was slightly move her left hand, and that was beginning to go?

But I knew the answers to those questions were in that smile. She had been in the grips of a ghastly disease for six-and-a-half years and she was still here, not just here but joyfully here, loving the day, loving her family. And that's why she wanted her story told. She wanted to share the physical and emotional tools she and her family have learned along the way. The journey she's on could be done with grace, dignity, and a smile.

After her prognosis at such a young age and with a small son to consider, Jenni—along with Jeff—had but one option: move forward. They dug deep for strength they didn't know they had. Innovative and Internet-savvy, they researched, experimented and created tools to deal with the challenges this disease brings. And though extremely difficult at times, they have managed to live a happy, relatively normal life in the throes of adversity.

CHAPTER 1
"I Awake..."

To tell my story, I'll begin with today. Let me introduce myself. I am a naturopathic physician, a fun and inspirational friend, a devoted mom, a loving and adoring wife, a supportive and caring daughter, and a proud big sister—currently trapped in the body of a rag doll.

I'm lying in bed; my mind is 100% functioning but my body . . . Well, let's just say my body does not get a passing grade.

I have been dealt a hand that quite literally was my worst nightmare. And now, living my worst fear has awakened me beyond my dreams. By embracing again and again the reality of my life—whether it be anger, fear, love or gratitude—AND surrendering to the beauty and wisdom that is life, I am not afraid. I am grateful.

Often, on a typical morning, it is still dark when I hear myself think, "I AWAKE!" Something our son, Philip, now age 10, would bellow as a toddler from his crib as soon as he woke up.

Thoughts come tumbling through my mind:

"Now what?"

"Is it morning yet?"

"My elbow hurts. Is it ok to wake Jeff again? It's time to flip me like a pancake. How many times have I already woken him? Should I wait a little bit longer so he is not grumpy?"

Don't get me wrong, my husband is amazing, but lack of sleep brings out the grouch in him.

I can feel everything. My motor neurons are affected, not my sensory neurons. If I itch and no one is around, I have to think like a Zen Buddha master and become one with the itch. Fortunately, when Philip is around, this is one of his "jobs" that he enjoys doing. He'll check on me from time to time and ask if anything itches.

But alas, I lie in bed motionless, acutely aware of my inability to take care of my own physical needs. This seems to be hard for people to wrap their brains around. As the mere act of lifting one's arm, or even a finger, becomes an impossible task, most ALS patients continue to be fully mentally alert.

Lest you worry, I must tell you, my middle finger has not let me down. I can still raise it off my lap to give Jeff the "bird" if he provokes me.

And on goes my early morning mental rambling.

"Damn it, I'm still tired!"

"It can't be morning, Philip is not up yet."

"But my body hurts. I need to be moved."

Finally, I concede and say, "Jeff, can you roll me towards the door?"

Sometimes I am at my wit's end. I am not suicidal; however, there are times when I think, "Are you effing kidding me? Is this really my life?"

I get so overwhelmed by the magnitude of the losses, frustrations of what I can't do and the constant readjusting to my new normal. Add to this Philip yelling in my ear and Jeff struggling to juggle the weight of our world; I have found myself daydreaming about putting a gun in my mouth.

At times I wonder, "Is it time to escape this fresh hell?"

But alas, I couldn't even lift my arm off the bed let alone lift a gun.

On the other hand, occasionally I wonder if Jeff has finally had enough? Is tonight the night he shoots me in the butt with a rhino tranquilizer? Or smothers me with my pillow? Or even worse, will he leave to get the mail and never come back? I'm happy to report he has not acted on any of my thoughts. In fact, he's told me he could never leave me. If he did, his mom would kill him.

You might be reading this and thinking, "What the . . .? That's horrible!"

Actually, it's our version of humor. Jeff and I share everything. We share our thoughts and feelings, and laugh a lot. This humor helps us not take ourselves too seriously. Even more, it defuses some of the intensity of our circumstances and saves us from the ever-looming abyss of this disease.

Finally, my day starts.

Balancing the roles of caregiver and father leaves Jeff torn rushing between helping Philip get ready for his day and tending to me. Philip's needs are many, while my most urgent need is for Jeff to transfer me to the bathroom.

There, I sit staring at the door, hoping Jeff will hear me when I attempt to yell out "All done." With every day that passes, my yell is diminishing into a faint whisper.

Once back in bed, after adjusting and readjusting, propping my different limbs with pillows and gel-packs until I am finally comfortable, my daily regimen begins. Jeff feeds me breakfast and morning supplements through my feeding tube, washes and moisturizes my face and hands, cleans and applies deodorant to my underarms, brushes my teeth and hair, plucks stray chin hairs, clears out my nose with a suction machine (since I can no longer blow my nose), as well as whatever else I need. Finally, we are ready to select my fashion statement for the day and get me dressed.

By some miracle, no matter how hard yesterday was, somewhere deep inside, my reset button is activated. Ready and open for a new day, I greet my helper-of-the-day and we're off.

CHAPTER 1: "I Awake"

Jenni (8 years, 11 months after diagnosis)

CHAPTER 1: "I Awake"

Philip, Jeff & Jenni
(4 months after diagnosis)

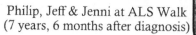
Jenni (16 months
after diagnosis)

Philip, Jeff & Jenni at ALS Walk
(7 years, 6 months after diagnosis)

CHAPTER 2

Part 1: Jenni, the Early Years

Before we continue on my ALS journey, here's some background on my life. A life that ALS had no part of.

Let's go back to the beginning. I was born in Cleveland, Ohio in 1976. My mom, Joyce, is from Maryland, and my dad, Elliot, is from California. Cleveland was their home for six years while my dad attended podiatry school. This was followed by a one-year internship in Indianapolis in 1979. Much to their surprise, an opportunity to purchase a medical practice arose that was too good to turn down. The fates aligned and Indianapolis became my home.

In 1980, my little brother Robbie joined the family. My mom always said that I was a quiet, easy-going child. My brother Robbie was a little more intense and active, but the two of us were very sweet to each other.

My childhood was completely . . . uneventful. I felt safe, loved, and provided for. I got along with my younger brother and academic success came fairly easily. The biggest event in my adolescence was my parents' divorce, which was sad, but at that time, relatively drama-free and civil. (The drama would come later . . . stay tuned.)

If I had one issue, it was the very thick glasses I had to wear from a young age. Those "optical bottle caps" exacerbated a painful shyness. I constantly wanted to disappear or at least become invisible. I was quiet and people thought me a sweet, nice, good girl.

I had amblyopia, also known as lazy eye, that was caught and treated when I was only eighteen months old. My mom told me that when I had my glasses on for the first time and could actually see, I looked around at everything in complete awe.

My poor vision and shyness molded who I was as an adolescent and teenager. At North Central High School, which had nearly 4,000 students, I found that I was more comfortable with a close group of friends. After experiencing such a large high school, I longed for a small college and found a perfect fit at charming Beloit College in Wisconsin.

During the summer of 1996, between my sophomore and junior year of college, my life changed dramatically. I attended a three-day seminar called The Landmark Forum. I walked away with a new understanding that my shyness was just a state of mind. The program, which focused on self-awareness and communication, enabled me to transform my social discomfort to an openness that helped shape who I am today.

Ironically, years later, it would be ALS that finally vanquished my shyness for good. Losing more and more of my abilities and becoming more reliant on others to be my arms and legs ultimately forced me to be a more vocal, more visible, more present personality. You can't disappear when you're in a wheelchair.

That life-changing summer weekend got me on my way, not only transforming my shyness but also igniting my passion for dance and performance. This passion grew and became a hunger for adventure and eventually catapulted me out of the Midwest and into the world at large.

I first landed in Colorado with Tessa, a college friend. The two of us were running on an indoor track in the cold Wisconsin winter of my junior year talking about summer vacation when I said, "I don't want to spend this summer at home."

"Hey, this could be great," said Tessa. "My sister and I need a third roommate to share expenses in Telluride this summer. Do you want to join us?"

I was in. The three of us rented a house on a ranch and got

jobs cleaning condos in town. The property was vast and horses grazed on the land. Cows from a neighboring ranch would occasionally visit.

As a temporary cowgirl, I learned some fun facts. Cows are not the sharpest tools in the barn. To get them off your property, all you have to do is brush them slightly with the bristles of a broom. They think it's a fence and move on.

The dogs on the ranch taught us about Mother Nature's defenses. When we experienced our first up close and personal skunk spray, we called the local sheriff's department. The smell was worse than anything we could imagine. We thought there might have been a chemical spill in the area. They had a good chuckle at us "city slickers." It was late at night and we were too tired to start bathing the dogs. Instead, we went to bed with our noses in jars of salsa. Next, the dogs decided to "play" with a porcupine and came back completely covered in quills. I learned that the needles, tipped with microscopic backward-facing barbs, had to be tediously pushed out one by one in the direction they went in. Ouch! Maybe this is why I chose not to add acupuncture as part of my naturopathic degree.

We eventually lost our cleaning jobs because, frankly, we weren't very good at it. I believe in a "lived-in" look. We were able to rustle up employment at a taco food truck during the annual Telluride Jazz Festival to make ends meet and had a blast doing it.

I loved every minute of my time in Colorado, and it sealed my friendship with Tessa for life.

After college graduation in 1998, we planned to move to the Big Apple. Who wouldn't want to live in an exciting city like New York when you are young and free? Me actually. Before embarking on our adventure, I spent the summer with my good friend Jessica who lived in the Bronx. That summer was long enough for me to discover even though I LOVED her and her family, I HATED everything about the realities of living in New York City—getting around, trying to find a job, the crowds. So when Tessa cautiously approached me with the idea of following her boyfriend to the University of Washington for his graduate program, I happily changed directions. The moment I arrived in Seattle it felt like home.

I settled happily in Seattle for three years and really began to see the world—the world of the aged as an activity director for Foss Home and Village nursing facility, and the world of refugees as a volunteer and donation coordinator for the Catholic Archdiocese of Seattle.

I truly felt as though I was a part of the global community and that I was offering a safe haven for people who needed it most.

I cheerfully drove the seniors to Mariners' games, on shopping excursions, and fishing trips. I learned to navigate the city with ease driving a giant handicap-accessible van. The residents were fun, funny, and interesting with a smattering of jerks. I sat with people as they lay dying. My first long-term job was incredibly formative and meaningful.

My next job was with the Catholic Archdiocese of Seattle in their refugee assistance program as their volunteer and donation coordinator. The group was young, hip, and supersaturated with idealism. I spent my days running around the city acting as my own personal AMVETS. One time, I broke down 15 twin beds by myself at a university and hauled the frames into my van. I met families from Bosnia, East Africa, and the Sudan. The Sudanese Lost Boys, who had been hiding from lions, dodging bullets, and subsisting on porridge, thought that when it snowed it was "raining milk." Between my experience with the nursing home and the refugees, I found a true appreciation of my youth and my good fortune.

Now we get to the love and romance, the hearts and flowers

part of my story.

Enter Jeff Berebitsky, who would become my future husband and the love of my life. It would take some time before I figured all that out.

Back in Indy in 1999, my mom was working in real estate. She had a client named Doug and it came to light that his brother Jeff lived in Seattle. Since we were the same age, single, and both Jewish, naturally, they fixed the two of us up.

Jeff was funny, fit, and interesting. We connected over our international travels. I thought Jeff visiting South Africa was very sexy. But there was a problem and it was a big one. Jeff had a mullet.

The next date when Jeff picked me up, he mentioned that he really needed a haircut. Tessa, now my housemate, said, "Oh! I cut hair," which was an untruth. "I can do it here." She led him into the bathroom and quickly cut off the mullet before Jeff could utter a word. Jeff took this in stride except adding, "Funny, usually when I get a haircut, they ask me what I want."

But mullet or not, we did not become an item. Instead, we became friends and stayed in touch. Several weeks later at a party, I met Joel, a fun, adventurous native of Seattle. After our courtship, Joel and I moved in together, living the dream of young professionals in the Pacific Northwest. When George W. Bush was on the ticket for the 2000 presidential election, we decided (partly in jest) to leave the country if he were elected. Sure enough, after many voter recounts and a court decision, the two of us moved to Australia.

Joel and I studied at Melbourne University—me, social theory and Joel, international relations. While walking to and from the classes that bored me, I became increasingly intrigued by the School of Natural Medicine that was so conveniently on my path. At mid-year, I switched my course of study. I knew immediately that I had found my bliss. I was completely in love with the material and the profession. It was as close to Hogwarts as I could imagine. For those of you non-Harry Potter fans, 1) What's wrong with you? and 2) In the world of Harry Potter, Hogwarts is the wonderful magical School of Witchcraft and Wizardry. I continued to study natural medicine in Melbourne for another year.

During the following year, I realized it was time for me to leave Australia. I was homesick. I had new half-brothers I wanted to meet, Joel and I decided we were not meant to be together for the long run and I did not want to get my naturopathic medical degree from a foreign country. Fast forward six months later, I was back in Indianapolis, and Joel continued to live in Australia.

I doubled down on my dedication to naturopathic medicine but needed some science classes before I could be accepted to medical school. Since I was in Indianapolis, I took my prerequisites at Indiana University–Purdue University Indianapolis (IUPUI). In the meantime, Jeff, who had been living in Seattle, also came back to Indianapolis and the two of us rekindled our friendship. Eventually, the spark turned into flames, and we became a couple.

I applied and was accepted to both Bastyr University in Seattle and the National College of Natural Medicine in Portland, Oregon. I chose Portland. In August 2003, my mom, who was always up for an adventure, and I were driving my ugly-ass nine-year-old Honda Civic named "Stanley" out west together. A year and a half later, Jeff followed.

Part 2: Jenni, the Early Years—Symptoms Begin

My life was rosy. I was in Portland, a city I adored, and was enrolled in medical school pursuing the career of my dreams. Jeff and I bought a small house together, a mere 950 square feet, across the Willamette River in North Portland. The cherry-on-top was our engagement in December 2005 and our wedding in September 2006.

My mom flew out to Portland to help me with all things wedding. The two of us scoured the city looking for the perfect wedding dress and finally found the breathtaking gown I would wear down the aisle. My mom spotted it on the "Designer Dresses Discounted" rack no less and took it into the dressing room, adding one more to the many silks, satins, and chiffons the salesperson had already chosen.

When I slipped on that gown, it looked like it was made for me. It was perfect. The pearl white raw silk gown with beading and sequins fit me like skin and would allow no room for dessert.

When I went in for a fitting a few weeks before the wedding, I was swimming in the once form-fitting dress. It needed significant alterations. On our wedding day, the dress grew bigger still. In reality, I had lost a lot of weight. Every bride's dream, right? Not in this case.

Emotional stress caused this extreme weight loss. Six weeks before my wedding, a very upsetting situation involving my dad emerged. The situation escalated. The more I tried to resolve it, the uglier it got.

I am leaving out the details of this "battle royale" on purpose. The only reason I bring it up now is to point out the unusual and rapid weight loss I experienced. Our family is at peace with the past, and I have no interest in dredging up the "he said she said" details. The "facts" are on a need-to-know basis. So, if you really need to know, call me and we'll sit down with a glass of wine and talk.

Now back to the story . . . the weight loss continued. The muscle loss, too. Leading me to wonder years later if the strain of the wedding and the emotional stress had anything to do with what was to be diagnosed in less than two years . . . or had ALS already begun to start its treacherous path in me months before I said, "I do"?

I call the months following our wedding "bulldozing my way through time." I got married, completed my medical degree, and became pregnant in quick succession, almost as if I sensed I was up against a deadline.

I was interviewing for residency positions in March 2007. One had gone particularly well. I asked Jeff to meet me at a neighborhood bistro that evening for a glass of wine to celebrate. We were enjoying the moment, the vino, and the festive atmosphere when I felt that wave again. I hadn't been feeling well for the past few days and I began to wonder . . .

Sure enough the day after our bistro bash, I found out that I was pregnant. Philip had been conceived on Valentine's Day. I had it in my head it would take me a while to get pregnant. It took one month. I wasn't sad about the news, but I thought, "Now what? What about my career? What about my residency?"

While I was a student, one of the residents had had a baby and it looked so hard trying to juggle both mothering and doctoring. I thought I could never, ever, ever do that. But I've learned that every time I say "never ever" it always happens. To my surprise, once I committed, I pushed through all my doubts and was able to do both.

Shortly after learning we were becoming parents, Jeff and I took the train from our cute little house into downtown Portland for a dinner date.

While we were walking along the street after dinner, Jeff started telling me stories about the misadventures of his youth. I started to cry after hearing them, wondering why I was having this man's child.

Jeff continued to share his escapades, clueless to the effect on me. As he told me, "My older brother Steve used to steal road kill and throw it in people's yards. The two of us would egg houses, play ding dong ditch, and make your basic phone prank calls," I wondered about how much of this man's behavior, my child might inherit. Next, some vague reference was made to some capers that fell on the wrong side of the law and the tornado/bomb shelter thing they had in the basement. This shelter became the new home for a lot of the family's canned goods. There might even be some Starkist tuna still down there.

But it was the "fortress of porn" that got them in real trouble. Barb, Jeff's mom, was so pleased that the boys spent so much time playing nicely together in the fort until one day when she actually peeked inside. She discovered the fort walls were covered with magazine pages torn from *Hustler* and *Playboy*. Needless to say, the fort was dismantled immediately.

After being regaled by Jeff's childhood memories on our promenade that balmy evening, I was beside myself. I told Jeff, "You never told me any of that! I was never like that as a kid!" But, alas, the die had been cast, another Berebitsky boy was growing in my belly.

As pregnancies go, mine was textbook. But the back of my medical mind kept nagging me about some unusual symptoms I was experiencing that weren't really typical to pregnancy. One of the first I noticed was when I was about a month and a half pregnant. I aspirated (a.k.a. down the wrong pipe) some horseradish at a Passover Seder. When the burning condiment entered my trachea, the muscles spasmed intensely, and it was so scary I had to leave the room to compose myself. About a month later, I aspirated some water. I thought this was strange, but my medical mind rationalized and decided my epiglottis had gone on strike during my pregnancy. For those of you who have not watched enough *Grey's Anatomy*, the epiglottis is the flap of tissue at the base of the tongue that keeps food from going into the trachea, or windpipe, during swallowing.

Even before I had become pregnant, another peculiar symptom had begun. I got winded easily. Going up a simple flight of stairs caused me to have to stop and catch my breath. I had always been in really good shape. I used to be able to race up the stairs on Mt. Tabor, but now a few steps were becoming a challenge.

At seven months pregnant, I was carrying a basket of laundry to the basement and fell down the last three steps. Luckily I fell into the laundry so I was fine. But again I wondered what was happening. Was it just pregnancy clumsiness or were my feet not working correctly?

I didn't waste a minute during these months—plowing through my pregnancy, finishing school in late May and studying for my medical boards with school chum Kate throughout the summer. We made it a full-time job. We met every morning and studied.

In September of 2007 I was beginning my residency at an out-patient clinic run by the National College of Natural Medicine. On November 18th I was bouncing on a large Pilates ball through labor pains that would go on for 12 hours. Philip was on his way and I was going to have him naturally and at home.

My midwife and friend Regina calmly sat on my couch knitting while I bounced and chanted "om." The meditative humming created a vibration inside me that helped me stay calm. Regina's knitting needles clacked right along with the chanting like a metronome.

"Keep it low," Regina said softly from time to time. As the pain surged my chant would naturally rise a few notches, and Regina had to remind me to lower the tone thus bolstering the vibration and soothing the pain.

Hours later, holding a bouncing baby boy, I lay in bed

marveling at what I had just accomplished. I had total faith in my body to do whatever it was supposed to do. I trusted it entirely.

I was going to feel very differently about my body 16 months later. But I spent the next six weeks of maternity leave recovering and enjoying my newborn son.

For nearly a year and a half, life was a blur for me. I was tired from being a new mom and a new doctor though I was able to juggle both. Contrary to what I first thought, with the help of a nanny and both my mom and my mother-in-law flying in alternately to help, we were able to manage it all quite well.

But my body continued to give me subtle signs of the disease that was destroying neurons in my brain and spinal cord, slowly paralyzing me. I attributed it all to being tired from being a new mom, or sleeping wrong, or a pinched nerve. It could all be explained away.

Snapping Philip's onesies became a challenge as my right hand became weak. It continued up my right arm to my elbow until carrying baby Philip turned into a task. I wondered if Philip was really that heavy or was I getting that weak?

As a resident I often gave group lectures to patients and others on heart and lung health at the Center for Naturopathic Medicine, a wellness clinic renowned for their cardiovascular and pulmonary care.

One day, a woman who helped organize the sessions asked, "Are you hard of hearing?" Of course I said no. The woman explained further, "You're slurring your speech the way someone with hearing issues might." I assured her I was not hard of hearing, but a chord struck in my mind. My voice was sounding different to me, too.

A friend who I hadn't spoken to in awhile called, "You sound weird," he said. "Why do you sound weird?" I panicked and went on the defensive. "I don't sound weird. I have a cold." But I knew I didn't have a cold. I just didn't know what else to blame.

Even my mom noticed something was off. She left me a message saying, "You have got to change your voicemail message. You sound horrible." I was initially offended by her comment, but the chords were getting louder—something was wrong. I was just not ready to deal with it yet.

The final straw came in a case of nerves that left me breathless right before I was to give a talk. My heart was pounding so hard I thought it would beat right out of my chest. This had never happened before. I might have been shy as a child, but I had gotten past that. I loved public speaking! I had always given these talks with utmost confidence. But I finally had to face it. The last few talks had been difficult. The anxiety that had continued to gnaw at me could no longer be ignored.

I turned to my medical school friend Kate. She had become a proficient homeopathic physician and had helped me in the past.

On a misty, gray February day in 2009, a month after completing my residency, I met with her.

"Aside from the anxiety, what else is going on physically?" Kate asked.

I told her, "Well now that I'm thinking about it, I am also having difficulty swallowing, I'm slurring my speech, and my right arm is weak." Listing all three of these symptoms together and out loud to Kate gave me pause, and then I immediately said, "Oh shit! This is not good." Kate agreed. This clearly had to be something neurological—probably MS, we both thought.

The idea of having multiple sclerosis was worrisome, but I had seen a lot of patients with it. They were doing ok and it didn't scare me. Besides I was otherwise very healthy.

Before I left Kate's office, I had an appointment to see a neurologist. It was scheduled for March 5.

Deep down I think I knew something was coming. For years it had all been just too easy . . .

CHAPTER 2: Jenni, the Early Years

Jenni, age 2

Jenni, age 4 &
Robbie, infant

Robbie,
age 3
& Jenni,
age 7

Jenni & Tessa
1998, Graduation
Beloit College

Jenni, age 20, Beloit College Dance Recital

CHAPTER 2: Jenni, the Early Years

Jenni, age 24, & "Lost Boys of Sudan" Seattle, Washington

Jenni, age 24 backpacking Cascade Mountains

Peanut Butter Engagement Ring

Jenni & grandparents   Jeff & Jenni
Graduation from National College of Natural Medicine
Portland, OR (1 year, 9 months before diagnosis)

CHAPTER 2: Jenni, the Early Years

Jenni & Jeff's Wedding
9/03/06
Portland, OR
(2 years, 6 months
before diagnosis)

CHAPTER 2: Jenni, the Early Years

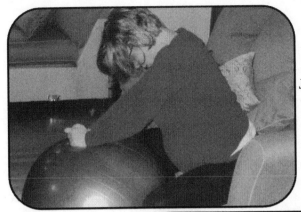

Jenni in labor

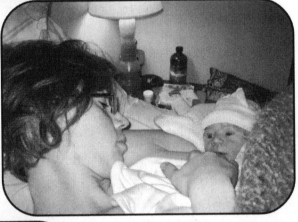

Jenni with Philip, 1 hour old (16 months before diagnosis)

Jenni, Jeff & Philip, 4 months old (1 year before diagnosis)

CHAPTER 3
Diagnosis vs Prognosis

Thursday March 5, 2009—a date forever emblazoned on my brain. It was an unusually sunny, pleasant Portland day and I was heading over to Legacy Good Samaritan Hospital in a bustling neighborhood northwest of downtown. I parked in the garage and walked the block over to the hospital, a list of symptoms in my hand.

From medical school, I was acquainted with the neurologist I was scheduled to see. After I went over my list with him, he had me put on a gown and meet him in the examination room. He performed a series of neurological tests—such as touching your finger to your nose to test motor skills, pressing your index finger to your thumb to test strength, and tapping various places on the arms and legs with a light hammer to test reflexes. The most telling test was when he observed my quivering tongue.

"It's MS, right?" I asked.

"Why don't you get dressed and we'll talk in my office."

Back in his office, I asked again, "So, do you think it's MS?"

"I don't think it's MS," he said. "I think it's upper motor neuron disease."

"What?"

"ALS."

"Wait. What?" I knew the disease as one that mostly affected older men. This was not making sense.

"Lou Gehrig's disease."

"Oh no. Shit," I said, stunned. I was only thirty-three years old, three years younger than Lou Gehrig when he was diagnosed.

Unfortunately the doctor, though brilliant with his quick and accurate diagnosis, was not blessed with compassion. While I dissolved into tears, he simply continued his instructions, telling me to go schedule an MRI with his nurse. The test would confirm or, possibly, rule out ALS, though the doctor seemed confident with his conclusion.

I know it wasn't his place to comfort me, but thinking back, I wonder if he had delivered the news a little more gently or perhaps asked if there was someone his office could call to pick me up, would it have tempered the horror of that morning?

I remember stumbling out to the nurse's desk, and making the appointment for the MRI the following day. In a zombie-like state, I found the restroom in the hall where I crumpled to the floor, bawling. Nobody said a word to me. They just stepped around me and left me alone while I cried and cried.

At some point I called Jeff. I couldn't drive my car; I couldn't even begin to tell him what was going on over the phone. I just asked him to come get me.

When he arrived and saw my swollen, panicked eyes he didn't ask questions. He drove immediately to my special place, beautiful Forest Park. It was my safe haven. It was where I often went when I needed peaceful surroundings to think things through. With 16-month-old Philip in a carrier strapped to Jeff's back, we walked the woodland trails under giant cedars and hemlocks. I continued to sob. I simply couldn't say the words.

Later Jeff recalled, "I didn't know what was going on. I gave her complete space to cry and just waited."

After 45 minutes in the fresh air I was able to talk. My eyes were swollen, my nose was stopped up, but I finally got it out. "Jeff," I said, "It's the worst possible thing that could happen."

Jeff had never heard of ALS. I asked him not to look it up on the Internet. I knew the horrors that he would find online. Something inside of me wanted him to stay innocent. Maybe if he didn't know the truth, this nightmare would not be real.

Of course, he did anyway. But even after his research, he didn't fully grasp the magnitude of the disease. It took a conversation with his mother, days later, for him to begin to understand: I would slowly, or rapidly, lose every voluntary muscle leaving me completely dependent on others. All the while, my mind would remain fully-functional, trapped in a motionless body, until the day I died.

Weeks later, he was given the name of a husband of an ALS patient to speak with. At their first meeting, the man said something unforgettable. "Jeff, welcome to an exclusive club you don't want to be a member of."

In the midst of all this, I couldn't call my mom. She was on a Caribbean cruise and wasn't scheduled to return until a day after I had had my MRI. Worse yet, I had kept most of my symptoms to myself. She was clear across the country and I didn't want her to worry. So, she was totally in the dark when she got home and called. All she heard on the other end of the phone was me, sobbing.

Within 48 hours, my mom was in Portland, and on Monday, March 9, 2009, Jeff, my mom, and I sat in the doctor's office waiting for the report.

"Your MRI test results are in, and they are clear," reported the neurologist who had given me the shocking news on the previous Thursday.

"Thank goodness," exhaled my mom as she sat alongside

Jeff and me in the office.

"You're going to be okay!"

We had gone into the appointment with high hopes that the doctor had been wrong.

The doctor looked at my mom, bewildered.

"You don't seem to understand," he said. "A clear MRI confirms my ALS diagnosis. ALS does not show up on an MRI, whereas MS or a brain or spinal cord tumor or even a herniated disc would."

My mom stared back at him, as if not sure what she'd heard. Then she asked him "What do people who get this diagnosis do? What's the treatment? What do we do now?"

Again he paused for a minute, perhaps surprised that my mom knew so little about this disease. In answer to her question, in an impassive, unaffected way, he replied, "They have 18 to 24 months to live. That's what they do."

Time stopped. The three of us froze in our seats while we struggled to comprehend the vast reality—and the short time— this statement contained. There were more words coming from the doctor, but they were incomprehensible now, like geese squawking far off in the distance. My mind started spinning in the void, an out-of-control top: I won't see Philip turn three. I will never practice medicine. What will happen to Jeff? What will this do to my mom? What's the point of anything?

The spinning stopped dead in its tracks when a thunderous rage rose from deep within. I may have been sitting there calmly, but inside, I was screaming. "Fuck this! This is not happening to me!"

Somewhere in the fog of words, we heard something about

an appointment with a neuromuscular specialist to see how far the disease had advanced. We walked out of that office like zombies. Our world tipped off its axis, our lives changed forever. We never saw that doctor again.

Within a few days, I met the doctor who would become my favorite. I adored her; she was so cool. She spoke to me as a peer, not just a patient, and was a great listener, open to whatever I wanted to try. Thin, vivacious, with brown hair, and a fresh, natural look, Dr. Kimberly Goslen, a highly educated neurologist, had the optimistic attitude I needed after the shock I had received just days earlier.

"We're going to rule everything else out first, because I don't believe this is what you have, Jenni. You are just too young."

Over the next three months, I went through many tests. One day, preparing me for an X-ray, the technician asked, "Is there any chance you may be pregnant?" I melted into tears, as I so often did during this time. I just shook my head and thought, "It doesn't matter. I wouldn't be able to have the baby anyway." I was starting to realize that my life plan, including my desire to have more children, was probably quashed.

After three months of testing, all the results re-confirmed that I had ALS. Dr. Goslen couldn't dispute it. All I could think of was the book *Tuesdays With Morrie*. Morrie was a cheerful, wonderful guy but he was trapped in bed; he was trapped in his body. Cheerful or not, he was trapped. And I most certainly did not want that.

During those first months adjusting to this new, now-officially-confirmed reality, I was as fragile as a baby bird. My mom and Jeff were extremely protective of me, screening my calls, emails, and visits. Corinne, my friend and Philip's nanny, continued to come to the house to watch Philip every day for a few hours even though I was no longer thinking about starting the career I had worked so hard to have. I was teaching GYROTONIC® exercise classes a few hours a week, and trying to distract myself the rest of the time.

Corinne's goal was to help keep the burden of my reality at bay. She would breeze into the house like fresh air and with books in arms announce, "I've got *New Moon*! I hope you're almost finished with *Twilight* because we've got three more to go!"

I spent my time reading the Twilight Saga, watching *Buffy the Vampire Slayer* (I wonder if vampire obsession is another symptom of ALS?), going out with friends, aimlessly walking the neighborhood or sitting alone in a coffee shop. I was hanging on by a thread. I was trying hard to live a normal life, but knowing I was dying had me just going through the motions most of the time. For months I would mood swing from denial to despair like a pendulum. And despair was winning.

By summer, I got help breaking through my melancholy and moving past my despair. I began to see my disease and my short life expectancy in a new light.

On June 25, 2009, Natasha, a close friend from Naturapath school; Melissa, a business acquaintance; and I were traveling down Interstate 5 heading to Los Angeles. It was a gorgeous summer day. News that the King of Pop, Michael Jackson, had died was announced on the radio just as our car was passing through Northern California in the foothills of the Cascades.

Surrounded by majestic sequoias and redwoods with a ribbon of sparkling blue ocean following alongside, we were enjoying the raw diet of veggies and grains Melissa had packed for the road trip. We listened to hits by Michael Jackson. His death may have marked the end of an era, but I still had mine. My sense of excitement grew as we drove south. We were to attend a workshop given by Les Brown, one of the world's leading motivational speakers.

A month earlier, my mom, Natasha, and I had been in Reno listening to Les Brown speak about his own life-altering situations. When it was time to get an autographed copy of his CDs, my mom approached him and shared my diagnosis. She then introduced Natasha and me to him. I think she was hoping for some magical suggestion to "cure" me. What he offered was "curing" in its own way. With intensity and compassion, Mr. Brown looked soulfully into my eyes and said, "Doctors will give you a diagnosis; only God can give you a prognosis." He then invited us to be his guests at his upcoming seminar, *Finding Your Power Voice*. We wholeheartedly accepted, and now, four weeks later, we were heading to LA.

There, we joined 50 other attendees who had also come to find their power, their voice, and harness it for the good. In one exercise the students were asked to come up with a quote about themselves that incorporated power in some way. After some self-examination I realized that my physical weakness from ALS was forcing me to be stronger emotionally and spiritually. At that time, little did I know how strong I would become.

The workshop also opened my mind to the idea that my attitude toward my illness could be powerful and, in fact, productive. If I looked at my situation differently, flipped it upside down and put a more positive spin on it, I could possibly profoundly inspire others. Something as simple as living as normal a life as possible with this disease could be inspirational. The idea I could motivate others gave me purpose. That was huge for me. After all, inspiring people to live a healthy life was at the heart of my studies; maybe this was an opportunity to accomplish something toward a congruent goal. It was in this seminar that I adopted what would become my mantra: "I had to get weak to find my strength."

Weeks after the Les Brown seminar, Tessa and I attended The Landmark Advanced Course, an empowerment training program. The leader was a petite redhead with a delightful southern drawl who surprised everyone in the course when she turned out to be tough as a drill sergeant. I credit her with nothing short of saving my life.

I remember that each time I stood up to share, no words came out of my mouth. All I could do was burst into tears. The Forum leader told me to sit down. Tessa shared that what she wanted from this weekend was to figure out how to deal with the fact that her best friend was just diagnosed with a terminal disease. She did not mention this friend was me. After attempting several more times to speak but still only able to cry, the leader said, "Sit down and don't bother to get up again until you can talk. You came here to get something out of this weekend, and crying is not going to get you anything."

I reached deep inside and with all the strength I could muster, declared, "I'm Tessa's friend."

At that point there wasn't a dry eye in the place.

"Jenni. Is that what you said your name was—Jenni?" asked the sergeant. "Jenni, you are a crybaby." The room fell unearthly silent.

I was flabbergasted. No one had dismissed my illness like this before. I had come to expect a degree of shock, sadness, pity, deference and after that, a whole lot of coddling when people discovered I had a terminal disease.

"What? But I have ALS." I didn't know what else to say. I was in the spotlight naked and hurt. Angry now, I thought, "How dare she call me a crybaby. This is a big deal."

"I don't care. You're a crybaby," the sergeant repeated even louder now. "Do you know how many people I've seen with a 'prognosis'? It doesn't mean a thing."

I continued to cry. But the sergeant didn't back down a bit, "When you cry, you are accepting a guess as the truth. You're letting this so-called prognosis define your future. There is no real truth to this. It's based on statistics, sure, but no one can tell you when you will die. No one! And when you buy into that, you fulfill the prophecy. And, by the way, everyone has an expiration date stamped on their foreheads—you're not alone in that—and none of us, not even you, knows what that date is."

The Forum leader went on to say, "Given your circumstances you have a choice: you can give up, accept your prognosis as the truth and 'die' inside, choosing to just exist until your body dies, OR you can choose to LIVE every minute of every day until you actually do die."

When I finally wobbled back to my place in the crowd after such a dressing down, I was a ragged mess, but my thinking had already begun to shift like tectonic plates before an earthquake, and an earthquake was coming. For the next three days I trained as if for war, ultimately ripping my prognosis apart and upending all that I had been told until I began seeing everything in a completely different way. Then I made a decision to forget what the doctors and statisticians had foisted upon me. I vowed to live my life and stay in the present and not give any more power over to the disease.

Through the course of the seminar, my perception of the Landmark Forum leader transformed. At first, I thought of her as a drill sergeant, but I came to realize she was someone who showed her deep compassion for others by courageously saying what needed to be said.

On the last day, she stated, "No matter what anyone got or learned from this weekend, one thing we can all agree on is that Jenni got her life back, and we were all meant to be here to be a part of that." As mean and abusive as you may be thinking she was, her brutal directness is what I needed to break through the wall of self-pity I was living in. I will be forever grateful.

It's been said so many times that it may sound hokey, or

like a cliché, but I learned that all any of us has is *right now*, no matter how much we reminisce about the past or dream about the future. We have this moment, and that's all. I decided then and there to make the best of it.

To seal this vow, the program encouraged me to "enroll my community in my new future, new possibility, and new purpose." So that's exactly what I did when this transformative seminar concluded. I called my doctors, occupational therapists, friends, and family—everyone in my circle—and told them about my weekend experience. I explained to them that I had accepted that I was dying but now was focused on living my life to the fullest. Even though I had no idea what that looked like, I was committed.

I carefully explained to everyone that I needed them to support this decision and agree to relate to me as someone who was moving forward with life—someone excited to take on what is in front of her—not someone with a terminal disease, waiting to die.

And it worked. I had my life back. The months of despondency were over. Sure I have my moments where I think this SUCKS, and I throw myself a huge pity party. But for the most part I have lived my life, just as I discovered I could in those workshops all those years ago.

NOTE: *The Landmark Advance Course is part of Landmark Worldwide which is an international personal and professional growth, training, and development company. A global educational enterprise committed to the fundamental principle that people have the possibility of success, fulfillment, and greatness. It is not affiliated with any religion. It offers tools for people all over the world, from Milwaukee to Nairobi.*

CHAPTER 3: Diagnosis vs Prognosis

Jenni, Jeff & Philip
Forest Park,
Portland, OR
(4 months
before diagnosis)

Jenni & Philip
(4 weeks after diagnosis)

Jeff, Philip & Jenni
(5 months after diagnosis)

Joyce & Jenni
Speaking at ALS Association event
(1 year, 8 months after diagnosis)

CHAPTER 4
The Life that Is Waiting for Me

*We must be willing to get rid of the life we've planned, so as to
have the life that is waiting for us.*
~ Joseph Campbell

Don't get me wrong. Off and on there were tears and some
heavy soul-searching for me to continue embracing this
philosophy, but I did. And once I did, I was able to move ahead
in the life that was waiting for me.

In August 2009, Jeff, Philip, and I stopped for a quick two-
day visit in Indianapolis on our way home from a wedding in
Atlanta. Even though I didn't think it was time yet, my mom (a
realtor in her past life) had found what she thought was the
perfect neighborhood for us. After a little convincing, we did a
drive by. Once I looked at one of the flyers for houses on sale, I
felt like I had found my dream home.

My mom arranged for us to see not just this one but all
three homes that were on the market in this neighborhood. My
"dream home" turned out to be not that great, but the second one
we looked at was love at first sight. Even though it was smaller
than we wanted, having a sandy beach on Williams Creek in our
future backyard sealed the deal. By the time we were on the plane
back to Portland, we had made an offer on this house.

Jeff had wanted to move back to Indy eventually, but I
wasn't quite ready. I wanted to practice naturopathic medicine in
Portland surrounded by my peers. Still, when we saw the house
in the woods on a creek, we knew it was time. I have always felt
that the house really found us or I guess truth be told, my
mother's persistence found us the house.

Then I took baby steps. That fall, I was a bridesmaid in my friend Natasha's wedding. I viewed my participation in the wedding as part of the momentum needed to keep my life moving forward, choosing to show up instead of giving up.

The same weekend as Natasha's wedding was a Walk to Defeat ALS, hosted by the ALS Association in Indianapolis. It would be the first of many ALS Walks that my family and friends would participate in. The Walk was significant in many ways, despite my not being there in person. It was my first opportunity to experience the community that would form and grow over the years. It was also my first chance to reach out and communicate with others. Now, it wasn't just about me and my inner monologue. It was me opening my soul to those who came to our first Walk to support and celebrate me. I wrote a letter that my mom printed and gave to each person at the conclusion of the Walk:

And now, a few words on health from Jenni Berebitsky, naturopathic doctor:

Health has been my life, my career and was to be my future. Six months ago, health became a convoluted, ambiguous headliner in my life.

Six months ago I had completed my residency in naturopathic medicine. I had completed my teaching training to become a Gyrotonic instructor. I had my career. I had my education. I had my 15-month-old baby. I had my husband. I had my home in Portland. I had my home in Indiana. I had my friends. I had my cat. I had my good fortune and my debt. I had my health.

Six months ago I saw a doctor. I saw a doctor who told me I have eighteen months to live. Eighteen possibly twenty-four months to bear witness as my body, slowly or rapidly, disintegrates by a fatal degenerative neurological condition, a disease that would eventually paralyze my body. My body that is still active and vital.

And then with active and vital tears, I cried. For months and months, I grieved the life I have lived. I grieved the life I have yet to live. I grieved my regrets and my fears that have paralyzed me before.

In six months, I visited energy healers. I got a counselor. I traveled the land to motivational leaders and speakers. I listened to meditation CDs during the nights that plagued me with the dusty bleakness of an unforeseen future. I saw naturopaths, homeopaths. I was on a path to deny what was ever said. Blind the fear with beams of hope. Squash any conclusion I might die before my son turns three. Prove that I will continue to live a long life that is on occasion paralyzed by fear and insecurity and not sclerosis of my spinal cord.

Before I saw the diagnosis-giving doctor, I had my health but never acknowledged it. Before I saw the diagnosis-giving doctor, I did visualizations for wealth, prosperity, success, and happiness. To me, the naturopath, health was a given. However with these words of a diagnosis, I glimpsed my own mortality and my consciousness of health was born.

Now, six months into my health journey, as the shock begins to settle around the unknown known of my unknown future, I ask what is health?

To an observer of my life, I am the picture of health. I carried my chubby baby to full term while working as a naturopathic resident. I sleep at least seven hours a night. I eat meat and vegetables, mostly organic. I am thin. I exercise. I take no medications. I eat healthy chocolate every day. I know which herbs to take when I feel sick. I know which homeopathic medicine to give my son when he is ill. And if ever I don't know, I know whom to call, my healthy friends. Yet, at age 33, I was told I have a fatal disease.

At first, I felt a peace, while scared out of my mind. I felt enlightened in the pretense we call life, which now leaves me in the quandary and irony of health.

I am not a hero. Most of the time, I wonder what my life is all about. I try to walk the road of my unknown future and I stop dead in my tracks. Moments are monumental. My work is to be honest, authentic, and compassionate with myself because sometimes this is harder than I can bear and sometimes it is a gift from God to be alive. My work is to be present and to remind us all of the urgent call to action to live the life we dream about.

The gratitude I feel for all of you is so great. With your time, dollars, and kind words to my family, I am given the breath for strength. I wish I were there with you today, but alas life continues, and I am standing in my wonderful friend's wedding today.

Thank you with all my heart. Thank you for supporting me, my family, and my mom, who organized one hell of a campaign! Thank you for supporting the ALS Association, which is a remarkable organization. We are grateful for your contribution to our lives and the lives of so many others.

With all my love,
Jenni

And so I continued on my path of moving forward. In October 2009, Corinne, Philip's nanny, went back to school and could no longer come to the house. I was okay. I didn't need her to distract me from life anymore. Philip and I spent time together going to the park, the Oregon Museum of Science and Industry and, because even at this young age he was passionate about basketball, hunting for hoops in the neighborhood.

I also added more GYROTONIC® classes to my teaching schedule and began giving wellness talks again. I did this despite my slurring speech. These baby steps became leaps and it wasn't long before my life took off. Soon I was busier than ever, the way

I had been before "the diagnosis."

I didn't have what you would call a bucket list but I did have a very extensive "might-as-well-not-put-it-off list."

One of the first highlights of my list was a trip to Italy. Jeff and I had missed the wedding of our friends, Karen and Alex, in Tuscany. But, as a wonderful consolation prize, we got an invitation to help with the olive harvest on Alex's family farm. November 2009, Tuscany was heavenly. This blissful week was like sleep-away camp with wine.

Karen, Alex, Jeff, and I, along with other friends, stayed in a 400-year-old house on a farm that hadn't been renovated in over 100 years. The chill of it almost wore off the charm because the only heat came from a wood-burning stove located in the middle of the hallway. Our bedroom was in the far corner of the upstairs. On top of that, the beautiful tall windows barely closed, which made it one very cold room.

Alex's Italian mama was very protective of me. She piled on blankets and sweaters to keep me warm and fed me lots of food to fatten me up. By this time, I was getting thin, losing muscle mass, and also tiring easily.

We worked hard. All morning on ladders we combed the branches of the olive trees, plucking off the fruit and gathering it into nets. At midday we stopped for a meal of cheeses, breads, and lots of homemade wine. The food was amazing. We drank a lot but managed to shake off the buzz for another four hours of work in the afternoon. Dinners included rich soups, stews, pasta, and fennel salad all made by Alex's Italian mama. It was a wonderful time, but ALS hadn't disappeared. A fall on a cobblestone road made me notice that my right foot was acting strangely.

Next on the "might-as-well-not-put-it-off" list, I decided to start creating my medical practice.

Moving forward with this idea was certainly not easy for me. In fact, I was all but paralyzed when I thought of my looming prognosis and my inability to know what the future had in store. I had Jeff's uncle to thank for the gentle push that got me off my butt and making things happen. Uncle Gary, a pediatrician from Phoenix, was visiting us in Portland. While we were out to dinner, Jeff entertained Philip as Gary and I talked about what was next for me in my medical career.

"Of course you're going to start a medical practice," Gary said to me. "Look, you have a four-year Naturopathic Medicine degree, and you've completed your residency. Don't waste it."

Once again tears—of both frustration and fear—poured down my cheeks.

"What are you scared of?" demanded Gary.

"I'm just not ready," I said.

I had been frozen on this subject and could not move forward. How was I going to get started? How would I handle the responsibility when I wasn't even sure what my condition might be? I had a lot of excuses . . . but Gary's was a forceful voice.

Uncle Gary's pep talk planted a seed in my head that would indeed blossom. It just wasn't going to happen in Portland where I thought it would. The Berebitskys were moving home. We were going back to Indiana.

In March 2010, nearly a year after that momentous March day in the neurologist's office, I was preparing to move my family from the little house across the Willamette River in Portland to the house on the bubbling creek in Indianapolis. I had gotten weaker over the year. Breathing was a little difficult, which zapped my energy, and I was losing the use of my right arm as the muscle deterioration was now up past my elbow. I knew I couldn't pack up the house by myself, so I asked for help. I made a schedule for the month of February, and for two hours a day, five days a week, one or two friends came over and helped. We packed books, clothing and toys; wrapped dishes and mementos until the little house was empty, and all our worldly possessions were heading east, including a very special hummingbird painting.

Our move would start somewhat of a domino effect in the family. Jeff's mom, stepdad, stepsister, and her husband would all move to Indianapolis within the year, giving us the solid and invaluable support we were going to need.

When I was first diagnosed and reeling from the death sentence I had been given, I sought comfort in the warm, cozy coffee houses that dotted Portland. My favorite was the Red E whose walls were lined with original artwork for sale by local artists. Now, in February 2010, when I was in the coffee shop for one of my last visits there before our move, I noticed a new painting, a resplendent amethyst colored hummingbird, its wings beating furiously just to stay afloat.

The tiny bird was painted larger than life on a canvas nearly the size of a closet door. I felt an immediate bond with it and wanted it to hang in my new home. I asked the barista who worked in the shop to wrap it. I explained how to wrap it securely for it was being moved with me to Indianapolis. This Portland hipster who couldn't imagine anyone leaving Portland said, "You're moving to Indiana? Why would you move to Indiana? Are you, like, dying or something?"

I was so shocked by this woman's snobby and inappropriate remarks, all that could come out of my mouth was, "Well, actually, yes. I am dying."

I took the parcel, thanked the woman, and left, hoping that this hipster had learned a lesson that day. Words do matter. As I walked past the shop and peered through the window, I saw that the barista's jaw hadn't yet returned to its normal position. I still chuckle at the absurdity of this situation.

In my search to find out more and more about ALS, I found my role model in a Chicago woman, Anne Marie Schlekeway. Anne Marie noticed her first symptoms in 2004. As her illness progressed her speech was the first to go. So she started a blog, "Kiss My ALS." This was the medium through which Anne Marie described, honestly and unabashedly, living with ALS. She used humor and wit to express herself while doing something productive with her disease.

I followed Anne Marie's blog and connected immediately with her and her experiences. Not only did I find her inspiring, but also we connected because she was a Landmark® graduate and on staff at the Chicago Landmark office. At first I was wary about reading her blog because I had read other blogs that made me sad. But Anne Marie was such a funny writer and so insightful that I just loved it. She was bold and brassy with a head of thick, auburn waves and a penchant for shiny red lipstick.

Anne Marie wrote about her fight to keep her high heels, even though she kept tripping in them, and having to use two hands to put on mascara. She was a powerhouse of a woman. I wrote her and we became e-mail friends. When Anne Marie told me about the fundraiser for ALS research she was hosting in February in Chicago, I was in.

On February 10, 2010, my first birthday after being diagnosed, just weeks before the move east, I was off to Chicago with three of my Portland friends by my side. Kate, Natasha, Amy, and I were all dressed up in downtown Chicago, sipping cocktails and munching canapés at a huge party to raise money for ALS. My mom and her friend Kathi drove in from Indianapolis. Family friends, the Rosensteins, and Jeff's cousin, Dana, showed up and surprised us for this gala. Music was provided by the band Anne Marie had sung with years earlier. To add to the evening the band surprised me with their rendition of

"Happy Birthday."

The main purpose of the event was to raise money for ALS research (ALS Therapy Development Institute (TDI) ALS.net). To accomplish this, Anne Marie sold iconic bikini panties with the words "Kiss My ALS" and a red lipstick kiss imprinted on them. Kisses and pictures with firemen were also sold. Adding inspiration to the evening, Anne Marie gave one of her impressive "speechless speeches" via PowerPoint. Her words mirrored my thoughts. We were clearly cut from the same cloth. She shared with everyone her beliefs of not giving in to fear and of living your life to the fullest no matter what the circumstances.

After the presentation, I went over to meet my hero in person. Anne Marie couldn't speak so she scribbled things on her notepad. She said she was very happy I could be there. Anne Marie introduced her parents to my mom and me. She was a cool lady. It was the first time I'd witnessed someone with this disease so empowered. It was the first time I didn't feel alone. Ten months later, Anne Marie passed away.

When I returned to Portland, I hit the ground running.

Jeff said, "I'm glad you had a good time in Chicago but we have to move out of this house in a few days so the painters can get it ready to sell."

Our Indianapolis house was also being worked on and would not be ready for another week. So we moved in with Alena, one of our Portland friends.

While we waited in Portland, the remodeling project for our new house was finished. Our boxes and furniture arrived and our two moms combined forces to unpack and set up our household. Once they did all the heavy lifting, Jeff, Philip, our cat, Asia, and I were free to hop a plane and fly across the country to begin the next chapter in our lives.

CHAPTER 4: The Life that Is Waiting for Me

Jenni & Jeff's Italy trip
November, 2009
(8 months after diagnosis)

Jenni, Jeff, Karen, Alex and friends from olive farm

CHAPTER 4: The Life that Is Waiting for Me

Jenni (far right) & friends at Ann Marie's Kiss My ALS Fund Raiser Chicago, IL (11 months after diagnosis)

Philip & Jenni in flight, moving home to Indianapolis (1 year after diagnosis)

Jeff, Philip & Jenni
(18 months after diagnosis)

Jenni, Jeff & Philip
(2 years, 4 months after diagnosis)

Jenni's last visit to the creek in her backyard. Carried down in her "flying carpet" by Rob & Jeff. (4 years, 2 months after diagnosis)

CHAPTER 5
My Inner MacGyver

The spring months of 2010 found us settling into our new Indianapolis home and acquainting ourselves with the neighborhood. That included having to explain my illness to people who, at first meeting, believed I was either from another country or hard of hearing due to my unusual speech. It was a routine Jeff and I would find ourselves doing over and over again.

As the months passed and my disease progressed, new challenges arose. I could buckle Philip into his car seat or stroller, but when it came to unbuckling him, I just couldn't do it. My hands were too weak. Without the help of strangers passing by, Philip might still be in his car seat today.

In spite of loving help, these situations left me feeling helpless and more and more frustrated. It was also becoming impossible for me to turn house and car keys in their locks, pull apart packaging, or open plastic bottles. My environment turned increasingly hostile as I became more debilitated. Time for another inner pep talk. I started saying to myself, "Come on Jenni, you've got to figure this out."

"Necessity is the mother of invention," and inventing is precisely what I did. I came up with ideas inspired by an educational theory developed a century ago by Maria Montessori.

Since he was two years old, Philip had been attending Montessori schools. This method of teaching is based on tailoring the classroom environment to meet the personality and needs of each child while promoting freedom and independence.

Jeff and I had organized our home with these ends in mind. This allowed Philip to do things on his own: dress himself, get his own snacks and dishes, and clean up after himself. All of this was to promote a more independent child. Montessori was a perfect fit for our family. Philip could do more and more as, unfortunately, I could do less and less.

I decided to adapt this philosophy to match my own situation. I began thinking of ways to re-create my environment to help me help myself, ways to re-work things in order to achieve more independence and success in my day-to-day life.

I'm always thinking. This disease turned on the problem-solving part of my brain or what I call my Inner MacGyver. I'm constantly analyzing and trying to figure things out.

My first stop was the tool section of the hardware store. I tried to find something that would best replicate the pincer grip done with your thumb and forefinger for turning and ripping, and other tasks we take for granted. I decided on lightweight Vise Grip pliers for gripping and leverage that helped pinch open buckles, turn keys, and open bottles. I bought a pair of sewing scissors for packages that I would normally pull open. I carried them with me everywhere. Deciding to put Philip in a booster seat instead of a car seat, even if a little early, eliminated the 5-point harness buckle problem entirely since Philip could undo the seat belt himself.

With the help of creative ingenuity (mine and some resourceful family and friends), life with this crappy disease could be a little easier. Once the issue of turning car keys in the ignition was solved by the pliers, I began having trouble turning the car steering wheel. A simple solution suggested by Kara, one of my new-found Indianapolis friends, was to order a trucker knob, also called a steering wheel spinner. The knob, simply screwed onto the steering wheel, enabled me to use my stronger left hand to steer the car and not have to rely on my right hand.

Getting Philip out of grocery carts and toddler swings added to my growing list of frustrating public challenges. I couldn't lift him high enough to free his dangling legs from the leg holes. It wasn't just my weakening arms. Others confirm that my darling boy has a strong gravitational pull; he feels much heavier than a scale says he is. Struggling to pry him out, I more often found myself asking a stranger for help. There was some relief when I started to use my thigh as a platform beneath the grocery cart seat. He could stand on my thigh and then hop up into my arms. The best solution for the grocery cart problem was to put Philip in the back of the cart where the groceries go and not in the child seat at all. From there, he could more easily hop into my arms. However, at parks, there was no solution for his release from toddler swings except asking a helpful stranger to come to my rescue until he graduated to regular swings.

On to other solutions for my weak hands. Unless I wanted to look like I'd been in an earthquake, I would ask a friend to put on my eye makeup on the few special occasions that I wore it. I had a signature stamp made to replace having to sign my name. My solution for managing zippers morphed into a quirky fashion statement, the first of many. Using lightweight key rings, I fastened the ring onto any zipper tab. Whether it was a coat, jacket, dress or boots, I was able to hook a finger into the key ring and pull up the zipper. My invention became even more beautiful when my mother-in-law Barb came up with the idea to add "bling" to the otherwise plain key rings. Old costume jewelry provided that added artful touch to my day-to-day fashions.

Philip was a big help. He answered my call and was great with zippers that I could not hook together myself. He also became one of the best earring put-er on-ers in the world! And when the mood would strike him, he even helped choose which earrings would go best with my outfit. When our opinions differed, his styling choice always outweighed mine. I like to think I'm training him to be a helpful husband.

My Inner MacGyver found endless opportunities to shine. Opening a wallet and removing credit cards with infirm hands and fingers was nearly impossible. I researched and found a wallet made by Hobo with big magnetic closures that I could open easily. It had roomier spaces for extracting credit cards and a clear window slot for my driver's license, which eliminated my need to remove it at all.

The kitchen re-creation started by our moving dishes to the lower cabinets for easier lifting and unloading a dishwasher, allowing me never to have to reach above my head. Sheets of tacky Dycem (non-slip material) helped me open jars and grip items securely. My ingenious engineer brother, Rob, made me a safe cutting board that was designed like a paper cutter. The knife was bolted down on one side to prevent it from wobbling and slipping off. This invention allowed me to continue preparing dinner much longer during this stage of my progression.

As I meandered along the path that ALS had created, Jeff and I made changes to the house. First, we replaced all the door knobs with door levers. Next, hand railings were installed alongside the front and back steps. In my closet, we lowered the hanging rods so I could get to my clothes more easily. Soon all carpeting and area rugs, which were quickly becoming tripping hazards, would disappear.

This was the beginning. My environment constantly changed and evolved as my illness continued its relentless march.

Until this point, walking and getting around had not been too great an issue. My problem areas were swallowing and speech; right hand, arm and shoulder; and difficulty breathing. But as summer of 2010 drew near, I noticed my gait becoming unbalanced. I couldn't find my right-left-right-left rhythm.

I had fallen in Italy and perhaps that's when it started. Falls were becoming more frequent. One particular fall while I was walking to Broad Ripple with Jeff and Philip left a major impression on both my knee and my two-and-a-half-year-old son. For months after, Philip would generously point out, "This is where my mommy fell," certain that I would want the event commemorated.

After that, I noticed I couldn't pull the toes of my right foot back into a dorsiflex, which is what picks your foot up. The muscle that initiates the dorsiflex, the tibialis anterior, had become feeble. Walking and balance are nearly impossible without the use of this muscle.

Always active and fit, I thought a workout routine would be a good way to maintain my muscles. This is where my careful study of the body did not serve me well. In retrospect, I think my logic was that I could out-smart the disease by "muscling through it": I thought I could trick my body into getting stronger by exercising. So naturally, I signed up for a six-week total body workout, otherwise known as boot camp. It was hard. It hurt. I was determined. I repeatedly pushed through the pain.

And, sadly, I pushed too hard. I came out the other end much weaker. And when I went for a check-up at the ALS clinic, I learned something that I had not known.

When you work out to build up muscle, you first break down muscle fiber. Then a normal body replaces the damaged muscle fibers with new, thicker fibers, and a bigger, stronger muscle is the result. What I didn't realize was that someone with ALS doesn't have the capability to replace the damaged muscle fibers, let alone form thicker ones. For six weeks I was unknowingly destroying the very muscles I was trying to maintain. It was heartbreaking. I had done a lot of damage and my muscles were not coming back.

Walking had changed. My right foot continued to flop down and I had to pull it up with my hip flexor muscles instead of the tibialis anterior. This movement of lifting your foot from your hip flexor to walk is similar to the way you would move if you had a swim fin on your foot. Someone at the ALS Clinic suggested I start wearing a foot brace, but my vanity would not allow for that, at least not yet.

One of the first thoughts that had entered my mind the day of my diagnosis was, "I won't see Philip turn three." This thought continued to rear its ugly head until happily, Philip's third birthday arrived. This was a bigger milestone for me than for him, although he was excited. It was cause for celebration. It was cause for a party. It was cause for a . . . haircut?

"You're not supposed to take the fruits from a tree that is too young" is the explanation of the *Upsherin*, which celebrates a Jewish boy's first haircut at age three. The haircut is done by a rabbi. The grandparents, aunts and uncles all receive a lock of his hair. The ceremony marks the end of babyhood. And in Philip's case, it also ended a head of the most adorable curls.

Jeff and I planned a huge birthday party/haircutting ceremony. However, leading up to the event, there was a bump in the road. The weekend before the party, we had brunch with Tessa, who was visiting from Seattle. The three of us and Philip ate at Trader's Point Creamery, an organic dairy farm in Zionsville, Indiana, that offered a farm-to-table restaurant. After lunch, we were walking the bucolic grounds, when I suddenly tripped and fell.

It was a chilly day in November, so I had my hands in my pockets for warmth. I couldn't get them out fast enough to break my fall. I landed flat on my face. Blood gushed. Philip screamed. Tessa scooped up Philip. Jeff froze, then broke into his version of the MC Hammer dance proclaiming, "What do I do, what do I do?"

As calmly as possible, I replied, "First get me out of the middle of the road."

Spitting blood, with a tooth broken off, my face badly cut, my lip busted, and an eye already blackening, I stopped Jeff from calling an ambulance.

"I'm okay, really. It looks worse than it feels," I told him. I was hurt and upset but wanted to stay calm for Jeff and Philip.

Later, alone with Tessa, I told her how worried I was about falling and what fresh hell I might be facing. "Jenni, you fell. You didn't die," Tessa tried to reassure me.

"But Tessa," I said. "I lost a tooth!"

A tooth, my foot, my hand, my arm, my speech—it was one more loss.

Eighty people were coming to Philip's party the following weekend and I looked like I'd been in a barroom brawl. It was time to call in the cavalry. On the way to an emergency dental clinic, we dropped Philip off at Barb and Charlie's and called my mom, asking her to meet us at the clinic.

As luck would have it, the dentist on call was a cosmetic dentist. I was in good hands. My mom hovered over the dentist making sure he did not tilt my chair back. As a former dental hygienist, she knew this would be much harder for the dentist, but she also knew that ALS would not allow me to swallow like a regular patient. Tilting me back could have caused serious problems. This dentist was wonderful. He complied with all my needs.

Before the end of the day, a shiny new temporary tooth was filling the gaping hole left from my fall. It wasn't perfect, but it worked. The following weekend I was able to graciously host the happy event with plenty of make-up and one fake tooth. Two weeks later I had a new permanent tooth that was almost as beautiful as the rest—and I started wearing a foot brace. I was ready now.

Uncle Gary's nudge in that Portland pub the previous year had borne fruit and I began to plan in earnest to start my medical practice. Part of me was still afraid to move forward on this, but Anne Marie's advice came back to me: "Don't give in to the fear." Also, I have learned that with this disease, nothing happens overnight. I wouldn't be here one day and gone the next.

___

In July 2010, I hung my shingle at Indy Acupuncture and Health Services, Inc., housed in a charming cottage-turned-into-clinic in the quaint Broad Ripple Village neighborhood, only two miles from my house. My practice grew fast. I did little advertising. People found me. I started giving Health and Wellness talks at one of the local coffee shops and for local business groups. I saw patients three days a week, women making up the majority of my practice. My passion was treating women with fertility issues. I also worked with digestive issues, allergies, and pain management.

I gave all new patients a full presentation of my philosophy on how the body works, the patients' responsibilities for their own health, and my basic treatment guidelines. Treatment included supplements, herbs, minerals, homeopathy, other nature-cure methods, and, of course, food. On this topic, I'm with Hippocrates, who said: "Let food be thy medicine and medicine be thy food."

To address my personal circumstances, I started every new appointment by telling my patients, "Due to the nature of my health issues, my speech and the way I move are affected. If you can't understand me, please ask me to repeat. I want you to hear the words I'm saying, not how I am saying them."

This was designed to nip any further discussion of my illness in the bud. And it helped.

Dr. Jenni Berebitsky was "in" starting July 2010 and would remain so for the next three years. I loved my practice. It brought me a lot of joy.

I had realized my dream. I had studied, worked hard, and trained for it. Fear tried to hold me back, but the habit I was creating since my diagnosis was to live for today. Tomorrow would take care of itself.

CHAPTER 5: My Inner MacGyver

Lambs wool elbow &
heel pads for sleeping
comfort (8 year, 2
months after diagnosis)

Zipper pulls

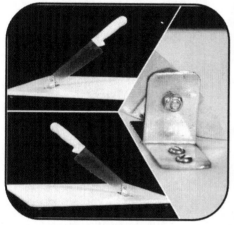

Homemade cutting board
Photography by Conrad Piccirillo
& Lisa Boncosky

Jeff, Joyce, Rob, Gretchen, Jenni
& Philip, age 3, eating cake while
getting his first hair cut at his
Upsherin, Hair Cutting Ceremony
(1 year, 8 months after diagnosis)

Philip, age 3 1/2,
Village Montessori School

CHAPTER 6
I've Fallen and I Can't Get Up

By the end of 2011, my legs were getting very weak. My fall at the dairy farm proved to be just the beginning of many more battles with gravity.

After the drama of falling and losing a tooth, I finally consented to wearing the AFO (ankle foot orthosis) brace. It was big and awkward. Even though it was stylishly decorated with butterflies, the brace was made out of hard plastic that went from the top of my calf, down the back of my leg, and under my foot to the tip of my toes. It greatly limited shoe choices and could never be worn barefooted. And though it helped a little, walking was still difficult and felt stiff, like trying to walk in a ski boot.

Fashion has always been important to me. It was and is one of my ways of self-expression. Brands are not important, but being able to make a statement with my fashionista abilities is my form of art. By wearing the AFO brace, I was giving up so much. I was 34 years old and did not like being told to "just wear sneakers."

Once again, I took matters into my own hands to solve this problem. I turned to the Internet, searching and thankfully finding that I did not have to reinvent the wheel. The solution was a brace called Foot-Up® that was soft and lightweight and worked with most shoes. They even offered a model that could be worn barefoot.

But you could not wear boots with the Foot-Up®! I loved my boots. Once more, I was obsessed with solving this new problem. I put on my MacGyver hat to figure out how to wear my boots and still get the support of a foot brace. With the help of a custom footwear shop in Indianapolis called The Shoe Fits, I turned my favorite boots into virtual Foot-Up® braces. A matching leather strap was riveted to the ankle portion of the boot and that was attached to the top of the foot portion, mimicking the foot brace. The result was a pair of "badass boots" that were quite the fashion statement and the envy of many of my friends.

Unfortunately, no foot brace completely stopped the falls. That year, I probably fell at least 15 times. I tripped on a hose in the garage, on the edge of the carpet in the house, in the hall closet, and over my own feet many times. But I always managed to get up if there was something I could use for leverage, like a table, or Piper, my ICAN service dog.

I must introduce you to Piper. A year earlier, in 2010, I had applied for a service dog through ICAN (Indiana Canine Assistant Network). Their mission is to train and place specialized dogs with disabled adults and children. The process is lengthy. All the puppies go through a year of general training and are then assessed according to their strengths. Once ICAN staff determine whether the animal is better suited for physical aid or emotional support, they go through another year of training before being matched with applicants.

These dogs are raised by meticulously selected inmates at various prisons run by the Indiana Department of Corrections. With the supervision of the ICAN staff, the dogs are trained by the inmates at prison facilities throughout the state. Amanda, Piper's handler/trainer, an inmate for 18 years, was one of ICAN's top trainers.

In June 2011, I went to the Indiana Women's Prison and met Piper, a beautiful labrador/golden retriever mix. Every day for two weeks, I trained with Amanda and Piper. I learned how to care for Piper, use established commands and teach her new commands that met my personal needs. At first, I did not realize that Amanda, was an inmate. She was personable, confident, and capable. I assumed she was a volunteer. It was heartwarming to see the difference ICAN made for these women. This program changes their lives, too. As ICAN says, "They make a difference on both ends of the leash."

When Piper came home to live with us, our three-and-a-half-year-old Philip was thrilled. He loved, loved, loved Piper. He would suck his thumb, grab her fur, and lie on her.

Piper was also a hit at Philip's school where the kids loved reading to her. This was one of my ways of contributing to Philip's school. We started in his preschool and made it through Philip's second grade year. Unfortunately, at that point I had to stop. I no longer had the energy.

Piper had been trained to pick up items off the floor, push the handicap button to open doors of commercial buildings, open household doors with a rope attachment on the door lever, turn on wall mounted light switches, and move laundry from the washer to the dryer, just to name a few of her capabilities.

She was useful to me over the next two to three years. I used her for picking things up, like my phone, and for balance when I walked. But Piper had two primary purposes. One was to help me up when I fell. I would say "brace" and Piper stood stiff so I could lean against her and get up. The other service Piper provided was acting as a buffer. Her adorable presence became an easy conversation piece, thus distracting others from my disabilities. I took comfort in always having somebody, albeit a furry somebody, by my side for physical and emotional support.

Piper helped me win many battles with my falling but gravity was to ultimately win the war.

And sometimes, nothing helps. Later that summer, Jeff, Philip, and I went to the community pool for a swim. Due to the heat we left Piper at home. Later, since I had an acupuncture appointment and they were still having fun, I said, "I'll see you guys in a few hours." I headed through the building toward the door to the parking lot. Boom! Over my feet I stumbled and hit the hard linoleum floor.

I was only able to get to my knees. I looked for a ledge or

anything to grasp but there was nothing. I struggled to stand, pushing weakly against the floor but it was useless. I just couldn't get up. The tears flowed. People passed me in the hallway but no one stopped. Maybe they didn't realize I needed help. They probably didn't want to embarrass me. They were probably just giving me my space, but it was awful. For several humiliating minutes I remained on the floor until someone finally stopped. By then I was crying so hard I couldn't get my words out, and they had trouble understanding me. Between sobs I finally said, "If you could just give me your knee, I can push up." And at last, I was on my feet.

It was one of my more pathetic moments.

A few months later, my friend Erin and I made plans to hang out. Erin checked in saying she had some things to do but would be there as soon as she could. I told her that the Butler Heating and Cooling repairmen had just pulled up.

"I'll just let them in and see you when you get here," I said.

I directed the men to the crawl space where the furnace was located. As they made their descent down, I turned to go into the living room but instead fell down on the kitchen floor. I was able to get to my knees but there was nothing around to grab. Simple solution: call Piper.

But this time, it didn't work. She wasn't enough. Not giving up, I walked on my knees to the living room to use the previously trusty coffee table to hoist myself up. But that didn't work either. No matter how hard I tried I just could not lift myself up. My arms and legs failed me completely. My phone was on the coffee table, so I called Erin. I was sobbing, I was so upset. Between sobs I said the first thing I thought of, "I've fallen and I can't get up." It makes me laugh now when I recall saying this campy phrase from an old TV commercial, but sadly, it was true. Erin said she would be right there.

Meanwhile, having finished their job, the repairmen walked back upstairs and saw me on the floor bawling.

The first guy rushed to me, "Ma'am! What happened? Are you alright?"

Flustered, the second guy just stared.

"No. I need help."

"What can we do?"

"Just lift me under my arms and help me to the couch."

Between the two of them, they got me up. I thanked them, assured them that I would be fine, and that my friend was on her way over. Then, I thanked them again and they left.

Erin arrived in a panic. "Oh my gosh! I've been calling and texting you, and you didn't pick up. I thought you were being raped or murdered." Then I saw that my phone had been upside down on the coffee table with the ringer off. Of course it would freak Erin out with worry when I didn't respond.

"Are the repairmen still here—still working?" Erin asked.

"No," I told her, "They left awhile ago. Why?"

"Well, their truck is parked across the street. At least it was when I pulled up."

She went to the window and reported that they were just then driving away. The men had waited for Erin to show up before they left so I wouldn't be alone. I was surprised and grateful. Kindness and thoughtfulness would continue to show up from the most unexpected sources.

Now, I had a brand new problem. When I fell, I really

couldn't get up. At least not by myself anymore. Not even with the help of Piper.

Since being diagnosed, I had shed enough tears to compete with Niagara Falls. It may be hard for others not living with this disease to understand the frustration, humiliation, and exasperation that come from living with ALS. You solve one problem and another pops right up. It's an unimaginable nightmare. And yet, though I have been sad and frustrated at times, like anyone else, I came to find out that much of my weeping was not about my struggle. It was due to a neurological component of ALS called emotional lability, also known as PBA (Pseudobulbar Affect). It can affect brain signaling, causing outbreaks of involuntary crying or laughing. It takes very little for an ALS patient to dissolve into tears over which they have little control.

I had been advised to take antidepressants for my crying. Dr. Goslen in Portland was the first to bring it up, and I was almost offended by the suggestion. I wasn't depressed! Of course I was upset. I'd been diagnosed with a terminal disease for heaven's sake. But as a Naturopathic Doctor (ND), in my mind, I would be a failure to consider drugs as a first line of defense. What would my ND peers think? My strong opinions far outweighed the benefits, so accepting Zoloft as a solution wouldn't come until years later.

Despite countless episodes of uncontrollable tears, it only took one comment from Philip to change my mind. One day, I was in the kitchen crying over what I can't now even remember. Philip walked by and said, "Mom, are you crying AGAIN?"

His question made me rethink the whole issue.

"That's it!" I said to myself, "I can't have my son remembering me crying all the time. What principles am I holding on to and at what cost?"

So I gave in, started on Zoloft, and the uncontrollable crying ended. Why did I wait so long? I learned to get out of my own way. Never say never.

Life with ALS is like being dealt a hand in a card game. The minute you've got that hand figured out the cards are taken away, reshuffled, and a new hand but with fewer cards is dealt for you to figure out all over again.

By the fall of 2011, my mobility had deteriorated to the point that life as I knew it was forever changed. Piper had helped, and I could MacGyver through some of it. But unlike losing use of my hands and arms where I could substitute teeth, pliers or scissors, losing the strength in my legs was a game changer.

The losses were many.

We begin with the hill . . .

We had been in the Midwest almost a year. Halfway through the cold, gray 2011 winter, Jeff and I had a chance to return to the West Coast and take a much needed respite in La Jolla, California, at Jeff's parents' condo. We felt fortunate to have taken winter breaks there, and we were looking forward to it.

The front of the condo overlooked the ocean. You could watch seals, pelicans, and surfers from the window. The coastal sights and salty air were exhilarating and good for my spirits. But the seaside town was hilly. In back of the condo, there was a steep incline that led up to the village shops and restaurants. The block-long hill had to be climbed every time you left the building. I had done it dozens of times in the past. But that year the hill was nearly insurmountable.

My lungs could barely tolerate the climb and my legs were pushed to their maximum. I was devastated when I couldn't get up the hill on my own. Weighed down by self-pity, I wanted to give up and just go back to bed. But instead I vowed to conquer it twice a day. Once in the morning and once in the evening. With people linking arms with me and pulling me along, I was able to do it slowly and strenuously. But the bottom line was that I could no longer just pop out and walk around town whenever I wanted. Another form of independence was gone.

While the hill in La Jolla was one of the first major sacrifices, dancing was the next. I love to dance! I was always the first one on the dance floor. But at my 35th birthday party, I found I couldn't move my lower body without tipping over, and I could only raise one of my arms over my head. I tried for one dance, I really tried but . . . I just couldn't. Once I had been a good dancer and it was gone. Even now years later, while I truly appreciate the ability my wheelchair gives me to get around, the dancer in me finds herself trapped awkwardly on the sidelines.

Next, I lost the beloved bubbling creek behind our house. It was a place to stomp and explore with Philip and to entertain friends and family. With its sandy beach, the creek was so very special to me. But my legs could not maneuver the uneven, loamy terrain anymore, even with help. It was just not doable, and I finally stopped trying. I watched from the big picture window in our sunroom as others enjoyed the creek. Feeling left behind and trapped in the wake of this loss, I would inevitably succumb to a pity party.

Contact lenses were hard to say goodbye to as well. I dreaded going back to the horrid optical bottle cap glasses, so I kept trying. But it was like playing darts with my eyes, with the contact lens usually missing its mark. Finally it got to a point that the pain was enough to have me give up. I didn't have many wins, but as it turned out, this ended up being a gain not a loss. Clear Lens Replacement surgery became the solution for this challenge. Goodbye glasses. Hello almost perfect vision. Being able to see without glasses was amazing. Why hadn't I tried *this* before?

Maybe not as dramatic, but still an adjustment, was not being able to talk with my hands. I was very expressive with my hands and when they stopped working I would often lose my train of thought mid-sentence. I'd have to say, "Hang on a minute. My hands want to do the talking and they can't."

An unexpected upset came with a 2011 Ironman competition. My brother Rob was training to participate in the one in Coeur D'Alene, Idaho, in honor of me and to raise money for ICAN. This loving gesture truly warmed my heart but secretly devastated me. I was an athlete and wanted to be able to compete, too. Ok, maybe not in an Ironman, but I knew the thrill of racing, and that summer I had to face that I never would again. I couldn't even go cheer my brother on because of my unpredictable physical limitations. The thought of navigating the Idaho terrain to see the various events had the makings of an impossible nightmare. Sometimes you never know what will upset you. What was meant to be an incredibly kind and generous gesture, was instead a reminder of all I had lost. (Sorry Rob. You know I love you!!! And I know you would never do anything to intentionally hurt me.)

Even something as simple as hugging had been fading until finally it was no longer a way for me to express love or affection—not with friends, not with family, not with my husband, not with my child. Picking up and holding Philip had already been checked off the list. He had wriggled out of my arms one time and I dropped him on the floor. That was that. I no longer held children.

As the disease progressed, the next to go was privacy. Due to balance issues and a non-functioning right arm, I needed help pulling my pants up after using the bathroom. In an attempt to stave off the inevitable, I had thumb loops sewn in my pants so I could pull them up myself and dress hooks replaced buttons on the waistband. But these measures only helped for a while.

Going hand in hand with the loss of privacy was modesty;

it had also left the building. I was still getting my period and someone would have to change my pads for me. It was so gross. Jeff mostly did this job and I was okay with him doing it. But when he wasn't around and a friend or helper had to do it, it was quite uncomfortable. The Merena IUD came to the rescue. Once inserted, my monthly menstruation stopped. If this hadn't solved my problem, another option would have been uterine ablation.

Another significant loss was that Jeff and I had always dreamed of a big family. At this point of my progression, we knew I could not carry another child, so we began to look at other options. We knew a young woman with cystic fibrosis who had two beautiful baby girls through a surrogate and thought this might work for us. We also considered adoption. At first it was just a lot of talk. And then one day, we decided, yeah, let's try this. We were excited and hopeful and decided to begin by looking into surrogacy.

Soon after Jeff and I decided to pursue this, I explained it in a session with my counselor.

"Why do you want to have more kids?"

"I really want Philip to have a brother or sister."

"Why do you want to have more kids?"

"I would like to expand the family, have a bigger family."

"Why do you want to have more kids?"

"Well, I just like a full house."

"Why do you want to have more kids?"

My counselor kept asking me this over and over until I finally replied, "It's just what you do. You have more kids—normal, healthy people have more kids."

When I heard what I just said, I realized the point my counselor was trying to get me to see. Kids are for normal, healthy people. I want to be normal and healthy. It was a harsh reality, but I knew in order to move on, I was going to have to accept it.

Even after the session with my counselor, there was still a part of me that clung to shreds of our dream. But a conversation with my friend Erin ended this discussion completely. She understood the cold, hard reality of the situation.

She explained "Jenni, you know I love you and I love babies, but if you have a baby, the baby's needs will have to come first. You would not get the care *you* need. What would that do to Jeff and Philip? How would Jeff balance everyone's needs?"

Reluctantly, I acknowledged she was right.

I then understood how implausible our hope for a bigger family was. It was hard to face, but it was the truth. It would have been unfair to a baby, unfair to Philip, and unfair to Jeff, and it would not bring more joy and happiness to any of us. The sadness will always be there, but I was finally at peace. A bigger family was not part of our future. Philip was going to be an only child.

But even with this peace, the realities of ALS leave grief under the surface. Years later when I was sharing this story with a friend, the rawness of the situation came to the surface. I relived the loss and began to cry uncontrollably. Unable to wipe my eyes or blow my nose, my mom intervened, becoming my hands. She wiped my tear-streaked cheeks and held a tissue so I could blow my nose.

My friend's instinct was to stop talking about such an uncomfortable subject. My mom understood and said, "Just give her a minute. She'll get through it." They waited for me to recover. It's horribly sad to witness such raw pain. But pity is something I neither want nor need.

For those of you under 18, "earmuffs":

The good news is sex still remains a part of Jeff's and my life. But with my limited mobility it's not as fun and free as it once was, and it takes a lot more effort and planning. I call it "comedy porn." But there's no doubt that we are a very intimate and affectionate couple. Seriously, this man wipes my bottom every morning.

As 2011 was ending, I had to add another loss to my list because driving became perilous. My leg muscles were unreliable, making response time tricky, especially dangerous on icy roads. Everyone agreed that I should no longer drive.

By year's end, what was left of my freedom and independence could fit in a thimble.

CHAPTER 6: I've Fallen and I Can't Get Up

Jenni sitting on Rollator walker (2 years, 9 months after diagnosis)

Piper & Jenni ICAN training (2 years, 3 months after diagnosis)

Jenni wearing Foot-Up® brace
Jeff, Jenni, Philip & Rob
(2 years, 6 months after diagnosis)

Custom adaptive footwear: (1) Leather strap added to mimic Foot-up® brace (2) Sandal, support ankles & allow for air flow (3) High boots, front slit & laces added
Photography by Conrad Piccirillo & Lisa Boncosky

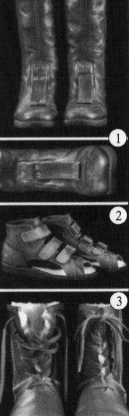

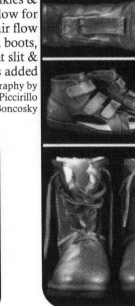

Jenni experimenting with wheelchair upgrades (6 years, 3 months after diagnosis)

CHAPTER 7
"How Can I Help?"

If there was a silver lining to all I had lost, I was going to find it. And as I tried to make sense of this lousy hand I had been dealt, a light began to appear over the horizon. I might not be able to "MacGyver" my way through every obstacle, but with the help of family and friends, life could be easier.

By the end of 2011, I was able to do less and less. Cleaning, cooking, laundry, and shopping had all been in flux, much of it falling to Jeff. But I still struggled to contribute to the family. One evening, I prepared a chicken for dinner—but then couldn't manage to get it into the oven. A neighbor had to come help.

It became increasingly clear that I should not drive, and Jeff and my mom could not handle all of it. Instead, they decided to turn to a community filled with family and friends who had been asking, "How can I help?"

The request was made and a new group, Jenni's Drivers, was born. Initially, my mom thought she would have to do all the coordinating the old-fashioned way, with a spread sheet and lots of phone calls. Thankfully, times have changed.

Erin found a website where friends and family could sign up to volunteer on a virtual calendar. Eventually, we switched to a more user-friendly site called *Lotsa Helping Hands*. We had dozens and dozens of helpers and soon there was someone scheduled to help me every weekday.

What began as a way to help me get around evolved into much more. We had so much help coming and going that Jeff thought maybe he should replace the front door with a welcoming revolving door.

The volunteers became my hands and legs and were willing

to do anything I needed done. You'd think I'd be thrilled. At first, I found it extremely difficult to accept their help. I felt uncomfortable, vulnerable, and bossy.

When I shared these concerns with my massage therapist and friend Donna, she told me about an interesting study. Scientists performing functional MRIs of the brain discovered that, depending on whether a subject was on the "asking" or "receiving" end of help, different parts of the brain lit up. For example, when someone is *asking* for help, the fear center of the brain lights up. But when someone is *helping*, the pleasure center lights up.

This insight helped me understand that I might be having trouble asking, but in a sense I was giving the helpers a gift of serotonin and dopamine when I asked them for help. It was time for their needs to outweigh my discomfort, and I quickly became a Master.

I was able to assess what people's strengths were and aligned certain tasks with certain people. My head-hunting skills were honed. I learned who liked folding laundry, who was more into food prep, organizing, running errands, "honey-do" projects, and so on.

I loved it. Who else gets to do this? Have one-on-one time with friends and family? And be around so much serotonin and dopamine without having to do drugs? But wait, I am on drugs. No, that came later.

I reveled in my life. To live a normal life is ordinary, while my life is extraordinary. I have friendships I never would have had and people rallying around me all the time. I had found the silver lining.

As the years passed and my needs increased, my helpers always rose to the occasion to learn what was next. This included many lessons: how to operate the ramps of our wheelchair vans, bathroom transfers, tube feeding, maneuvering and driving my wheelchair. The "courses" were taught by physical therapists, occupational therapists, Jeff, and my mom. We affectionately call these lessons CJEs (Continuing Jenni Education).

NOTE: *We have had three different wheelchair accessible vans as our needs as a family have changed. See Appendix B: Tips and Tools.*

By early 2012, it was becoming clear that along with driving help, I needed more help walking. Even Piper could not give me the amount of support I needed. I tried walkers at Costco and was delirious.

"This is awesome!" I cheered as I gripped the walker and virtually sailed through the warehouse. It was freeing to be able to walk with confidence, and having something to hold on to enabled me to walk at a good clip.

My brother was visiting at the time, and he, my mom, and I walked around the neighborhood. They couldn't keep up with me!

"Take that, Ironman!"

The Rollator was my walker of choice. It had a padded seat attached so I always had a place to sit down. Even nicer, the ALS Association of Indiana, like most ALS associations in big cities, had an equipment loan closet where I could borrow a walker free of charge. They even let me have two walkers, one for the car and one for the house. It was so nice to not have to lug one back and forth. The loan closet came in handy for many things in the future.

My awesome walker was used in conjunction with a push wheelchair (also borrowed from the loan closet). The wheelchair helped for longer distances, but it was the opposite of awesome. I had to rely on someone to push me because my arms were too weak. This gave me no real control of my movements. I would often be stuck facing a corner or wall whenever the pusher got distracted. I developed a real empathy for unhappy babies in strollers. And like most babies I saved the tantrums for my mom.

In the wintry months of early 2012, as we started planning for our annual getaway in sunny La Jolla, I worried.

"But, that hill, Jeff," I moaned. "People are going to have to lug me up that hill. Ugh!"

I feared the push wheelchair would be useless on that terrain.

A surprise was waiting for me when we arrived. My mother-in-law Barb had rented a power wheelchair. We didn't realize it then but we could have saved money by borrowing one from the local ALS loan closet.

The Jazzy® became my chariot to freedom. I situated myself in the chair that first day and was experimenting with levers and buttons when, before I knew it, I was racing down the sidewalk like a bat out of hell and ran it off into the grassy berm.

"Oh great!" I thought, "What have I gotten myself into!" But after getting pulled out, I got that bad boy rolling again and was soon handling it like a pro. The hill that took 15 minutes to climb the year before, I did in two minutes flat. I kicked that hill's ass! A whole new world opened up to me.

Tessa and her husband were visiting with us in La Jolla that year. As we did every year, she and I went for walks around the neighborhoods. Strolling through a senior living center not far from the condo, the residents there were impressed when they saw my wheelchair.

"Ohhh! Nice Jazzy," they hailed enviously as we passed. Tessa and I continued our journey while laughing hysterically.

I dashed up and down the little seaside town's once-invincible hills. Philip also loved riding on my lap. The phrase "confined to a wheelchair" is so misinformed. In fact, you're given the power of a wheelchair. People marveled at how quickly I was able to maneuver my wheelchair with complete ease. Turns out, I was born to drive six wheels.

When I returned from La Jolla, I gladly returned the push chair to the ALS loan closet and borrowed a power chair. I used this time to investigate what features and which brand I would ultimately buy.

NOTE: *Many insurance policies will only pay for one wheelchair every five years, so plan carefully. Make sure you get one that will meet your changing needs. The Jazzy would NOT have!*

A wheelchair brings its own set of issues, and I soon became all too aware of the plight of the handicapped. Bumpy or cracked sidewalks; roots growing through the cement; no curb cuts; these things made getting around problematic.

And stairs. So many stairs, so few ramps. We took our six-foot aluminum ramp with us everywhere in our new wheelchair van, but the ramp could only safely be used on a maximum of two steps.

Charlie, Jeff's stepdad, came to the rescue. He knew two handymen looking for work, so he called Jeff to see if we could use them around our house. Our first reaction was to say no thank you. But in a MacGyver moment, we realized homes of friends and family could use ramps. The decision was made. Let them build ramps! If family members and friends had built-in ramps at their homes, visiting them would become easier and more spontaneous.

So we made a list of "ramp-worthy" people. Our parents, siblings, and friends, those who might be interested in these custom-made ramps. The handymen were unemployed no

---

longer. Jeff's brother and sister-in-law, Doug and Kim, won the prize for their 64-foot ramp built up to their back door. We call it the "expressway." Jeff's sister and brother-in-law, Kylea and David, still hold the title for The Most Creative Ramp (a.k.a. the scariest and most treacherous, the one least likely for my mom to watch me descend without terror).

The irony of life in a wheelchair is that **you** as a person may become invisible but the wheelchair will always demand attention. The first time I encountered this happened when we were attending a concert at Clowes Memorial Hall, or as I nicknamed it, "Clueless Hall."

Lisa, Kara, Erin, and I were waiting to be seated in the handicap section on the main floor, but there was already a wheelchair there. While the ushers were working this out, I was left sticking out in the aisle. Suddenly I felt my chair heave forward a bit as a woman attempted to squeak past. She had tried to move the chair out of her way, but the chair was too heavy to budge. Now, if an able-bodied person were in your way would you try to pick them up and move them? No, you would say "Excuse me." Unfortunately this was one of many, "I can't believe they just did that," moments. "Wheelchair thoughtlessness," is what I call it.

I'm often amazed at how people recklessly dart to and fro across the path of my moving wheelchair. I need to quickly stop or maneuver out of the way. They don't seem to realize I'm driving a 400-pound bulldozer and could do a lot more damage to them than to myself. Isn't it the rule that the bigger boat gets the right-of-way?

Another major annoyance is that people assume if you are in a wheelchair, you can neither talk nor think for yourself. Often, when I'm in a store, people will ask my helper questions as opposed to directing the questions to me. A common question is, "Does she need help?" Ask me! I'll tell you.

Unfortunately people associate the wheelchair with cognitive or intellectual disability. An example of this is when my mom and I were at an event at our temple. My mom asked me if I wanted anything to eat. I said no. She then went to get some food for herself. When she returned, a "helpful" congregant reported to her, "She wants some cheese."

My mom said, "No she doesn't," but the person replied, "Yes she does! I asked her if she wanted cheese and she smiled."

I had smiled one of my sweet, polite smiles that meant, "Thanks, but no thanks, and you can go away now."

Instead this person, assuming I was "slow," interpreted the smile as if I was happy and excited about the possibility of cheese. She even looked at me again while nodding her head and saying in a loud voice, "You wanted some cheese, yes?" Seriously!

A silly not-intended-to-affect-me limitation is when people decide to use me as a coffee table and place their drink on the armrest of my wheelchair. This renders me "chair-alyzed." Unless I want to spill the drink, I have to gently remind them, "I am not furniture. Come get your drink."

Another funny anecdote happened when I was still driving. Piper, my service dog, and I were in a Target parking lot when two other cars had a minor fender-bender. I was in the process of getting into the driver's side of the car and the loud noise startled me. A concerned woman saw my reaction and came over to see if I was all right. After I told her I was fine, the women noticed Piper, with her ICAN service vest on. The women proceeded to ask me if I was blind. Duh! I was alone, except for Piper, and getting into the driver's side of the car! Yes, service dogs are amazing, but they don't drive. At least not yet.

On the other end of the spectrum, sometimes kindness and generosity show up in the most unexpected ways. While we were in Boston in 2014, Jeff, Philip, and I had plans to meet friends at a restaurant on the Charles River. Unbeknownst to us, there was construction going on outside the building and much of the walk leading to the door had been obliterated. I had no path to enter the restaurant. A couple of kind workmen noticed my dilemma and quickly got together to dump dirt and pack it down to create a makeshift walkway that could accommodate me and my wheelchair. Angels can appear out of nowhere. I definitely bring out the greatness and the weirdness in people.

Angels would appear again at my 20th high school reunion. The reunion was to be held at the Red Room in Broad Ripple Village. The Red Room is on the second floor of a building with no elevator and only a steep outdoor metal staircase for access.

How in the world was I going to get a 400-pound wheelchair up there? When I first learned of the venue choice, I was distraught and my friends were angry. They requested that the venue be changed, but it was too late.

After another pity party, I woke up with an epiphany. "I am not a victim."

The choice was mine. I could choose not to attend or have some of my willing and able friends carry me up the stairs. The latter would have me spend the entire evening in a push wheelchair. Confining but doable.

Neither option was acceptable for Matt, my Permobil representative (my wheelchair brand of choice). He understood what a power wheelchair means to a person. It is an extension of their own bodies or, as I call it, "my exoskeleton." He was committed to making it work! Hours before the party, he arranged to have an identical chair brought to the venue. With the help of one of his associates, they took it apart, carried it up piece by piece to the bar, and then reassembled it. That evening, five of my high school friends carried me up the stairs to the bar where the temporary chair was ready and waiting for me. To get me up the stairs they put me in a sling-like carrier made out of canvas with handles along the edges that I called my "flying carpet."

Thanks to the kindness of so many, I was able to attend, be independent, and enjoy my reunion. It was great except for a new problem: in large crowds, people could not hear me. This needed to be remedied before my next big event. Through research and trial and error, I finally found a voice amplifier and microphone that worked for me.

A disappointing aspect of life in a wheelchair is adjusting to the new height from which you experience the world. It can bring an unexpected feeling of isolation. I noticed this at one of the first family gatherings I attended in my newly borrowed wheelchair. Adults tend to stand up and talk to each other, thus towering over me. Parents and kids tend to sit on the floor with puzzles and games far below me. You're never at the right height and it's lonely in the middle.

There is a solution, though not paid for by insurance. It is a wonderful add-on feature, the ability for the wheelchair to elevate to the average standing adult height. If you can afford it, it's well worth it.

One thing is certain—I am always noticed. I can't go anywhere in my wheelchair and expect to blend in with the crowd. Little kids love this thing. I am covered in buttons, gadgets, and wheels. And I can go fast. Kids will often say, "You're so lucky!" They are too innocent to understand the irony.

And of course, Philip quickly learned how to turn my wheelchair on and off. If he's in trouble and I'm going after him, he'll turn it off. He knows I can't turn it back on myself. Like any kid, he can "push my buttons," but literally. It really pisses me off!

When I think about it, it's interesting how easily, even

happily, I accepted life in a wheelchair when not long before I had such a hard time coming to terms with a foot brace.

It's not like I was, "Hooray! A wheelchair!" It was more like, "Holy shit! I'm in a wheelchair."

I made myself look at it as a tool, like using scissors to open packages or a pair of pliers to open bottled water, to help me remain independent rather than as another step in my demise. I still wince when I look in a full-length mirror and see that person in a wheelchair.

Ironically, the foot brace was a much bigger hurdle for me than my overweight, unwieldy wheelchair. Maybe the brace, though tiny in comparison, was the first time I needed aid for my ALS-doomed body, and I was not yet ready. Plus, who the hell tells a 34-year-old fashion-loving woman she can only wear sneakers? Anyhow, by the time I sat in my first wheelchair, I was simply thinking of it as "the next thing." I had made peace with my evolving disease and ever-changing landscape. Necessity was making me a master at rolling with the punches.

But I still haven't and won't give up on fabulous shoes.

CHAPTER 7: "How Can I Help?"

Rob pushing Jenni
Indianapolis ALS Walk 2011
(2 years, 6 months after diagnosis)

Jenni & Piper going for a walk
(5 years, 5 months after diagnosis)
Photography: IndyStar/USA Today Network

North Central High School
20-year reunion
(5 years, 6 months after diagnosis)

Covered in hand towels after
being drenched from a sudden
downpour when dropping
Philip off at summer camp
(8 years, 3 months
after diagnosis)

Jenni & her brothers:
Asher, Rob, Alec & Ari
(5 years, 8 months
after diagnosis)

CHAPTER 7: "How Can I Help?"

(8 years, 10 months after diagnosis)   (8 years, 2 months after diagnosis)

Philip & Piper—there to lend a helping hand and a little bit of loving!

Philip putting earrings on Jenni
(8 years, 11 months after diagnosis)

Using the elevator option on
wheelchair, now eye-level
with other guests
(8 years, 10 months
after diagnosis)

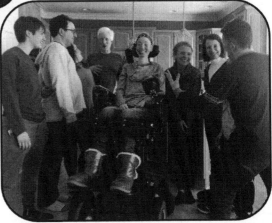

CHAPTER 7: "How Can I Help?"

Ramps

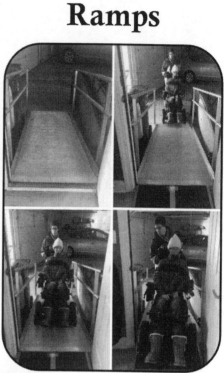

(1) Removable wood ramp built for front door
(2) Ramp & guardrails added to an existing deck
(3) Landing added to eliminate steps between living room and bedroom; ramp added to access step down sunroom

CHAPTER 7: "How Can I Help?"
Thank You Party for Jenni's Villagers

- Took a picture of Jenni in van
- Enlarged and mounted on foam board
- Cut out an opening in the driver's window
- Took picture of each guest "driving" Jenni
- Cropped and mounted pictures on a souvenir card for each Villager

(photo of real Jenni)

(cardboard images of Jenni)

CHAPTER 8
Decisions, Decisions, So Many Decisions

My decisions do not happen in a vacuum. Initially, I gleaned much of the needed information from helpful friends and caring strangers, as well as the Internet: Google searches, Facebook posts, the Patients Like Me website and other social media. Movies and books by others with ALS added to my toolbox of information when making life-changing choices.

Early in my progression, in the fall of 2010, through Jeff's research and a caring stranger who reached out through Facebook, a new procedure was introduced to us. Chronic Cerebrospinal Venous Insufficiency (CCSVI) is a term coined by Dr. Paolo Zamboni of the University of Ferrara in Italy. CCSVI describes a theory in which the veins in the head and neck are narrowed or blocked and therefore unable to efficiently remove blood from the central nervous system. When reviewing MRIs, he concluded that MS (Multiple Sclerosis) appeared to be more of a "plumbing" problem than a neurological one.

He found people with MS had insufficient outflow of blood from their brain. Dr. Zamboni designed a procedure similar to an angioplasty, but instead of stretching arteries, the veins of the neck are stretched. In 2010, there were only a handful of doctors in the US trained in this procedure. We found one in Atlanta, Georgia. Initially they do an ultrasound to confirm the CCSVI diagnosis, and I was the first ALS patient to have this done. I was hoping for a miracle as had been the case with so many MS patients.

Can I call my results a miracle? Maybe? I believe the CCSVI procedure slowed the deterioration of my speech and swallowing *and* eliminated my headaches.

In addition, I also believe one other non-conventional treatment significantly changed the trajectory of the progression of my disease. I continue to take, to this day, an off-label dosage of Naltrexone (LDN), which I began in February 2010.

NOTE: *These are my personal observations and do not constitute definitive medical conclusions. More information on both can be found in Appendix C.*

On September 11, 2012, Jeff and I were off to Boston to meet with Dr. Merit Cudkowicz, director of the ALS Clinic at Massachusetts General Hospital. We had heard about several promising new studies that she was heading and wanted to meet with her. The good news was that my disease progression, relative to that experienced by other-patients, was slow. But the bad news was that since my progression was slow, I did not qualify to be part of any of the studies. Although we left disappointed, we were still glad we went.

Meeting Dr. Merit was uplifting because she was the first neurologist who thought so far out-of-the-box. Her mindset was more cure-oriented than "deterioration management," which had been our experience up until then. We walked away with a list of recommended supplements. Although not FDA approved for ALS, Dr. Merit felt the potential results were worth adding to my regimen.

At that point I was using my power wheelchair almost exclusively, but we assumed we would not be able to bring it on a plane so we left it at home. Instead, we brought a transfer push wheelchair I had. It folded easily and was lightweight due to its little wheels and cloth back and seat. This was fabulous for the smooth surfaces at the airport but the exact opposite on the charming, narrow cobblestone sidewalks of Boston.

Jeff and I arrived a day before our appointment to get acclimated and decided to see the sites of Boston en route to a movie. Our leisurely walk from our hotel to the theater turned into a bumpy, vibrating, uphill, stressful experience. We thought relief would come at the park we were planning on cutting through as well as giving Piper a much needed break. To our dismay, upon arriving at the park we were greeted with two flights of stairs and no ramp in sight. You are kidding me, right? No, in older cities handicap accessibility does not seem to be the norm.

Although it would not have helped with the stairs-only park entrance, the cobblestone sidewalks or lack of curb-cuts, we decided then and there that we would never travel without my power wheelchair again. We reached out to a friend of my mom's, a paraplegic, to ask her how she does it. She "walked" us through the ins and outs of airplane travel in a wheelchair, so I was never again stranded without my power wheels. See Appendix B for more travel details.

An idea for my future self had been planted at the Heartland Film Festival in fall 2012 when my mom, Lisa, Kathi, and I saw the movie, *Jason Becker: Not Dead Yet*. Jason Becker was a former rock guitarist with the David Lee Roth band who was diagnosed with ALS in 1990 at the age of 19. Given three to five years to live, the only question he asked was, "Am I going to be able to tour?" No, he was not.

Within a couple years of his diagnosis, he was completely paralyzed, dependent on a ventilator and feeding tube, and unable to speak. He has lived this way for over 25 years. He continues to pursue his passion, composing music using a computer program developed by his father and uncle. He communicates with the computer through his eye gaze and movement of his chin.

He is surrounded by the loving support of family and friends. Once, a friend of his looked at Jason's prepared feeding tube food and said, "This stuff will kill you." In an effort to create the best quality of life for him, she created a concoction of healthy food and supplements that Jason could consume through this tube. His weight and color are the best of any ALS patient his doctors have seen.

It was inspiring to see someone defy the odds, forgoing the usual "doctor recommended" packaged food and instead, having his own food made in a regular kitchen using natural, healthy ingredients. Knowing that I was considering a feeding tube, my mom connected to Jason through Facebook and found out more about his diet. Being a naturopath, I knew a lot of the benefits of what he was taking, but it was still good to see how someone else was implementing this change in eating.

While some like Jason chose every life-saving measure, others do not. Susan Spencer-Wendel was diagnosed in 2011 at age 43. Before she died in 2014, she wrote her memoir, *Until I Say Goodbye,* about living joyfully with ALS. She had her bucket list of what she wanted to do with every significant person in her life. She lived the years she had to their fullest but chose not to intervene in the natural progression of her ALS. She declined a feeding tube and a ventilator. She wrote about her various adventures using only her right thumb to type on her iPhone. Her account of these experiences became her heart-warming book about living a lifetime in three years.

I had not had a role model since Ann Marie. With humor and thoughtfulness Susan put into words what I was experiencing day to day. So much of how Susan was choosing to live her life resonated with me except one choice. Weighing what I learned from Jason's movie and Susan's book, my decisions became very clear. I wanted a feeding tube but not a ventilator.

In 2012, I could still feed myself but had to use my left hand since my right one didn't function anymore. I couldn't cut up my food, so Jeff cut it for me at home. In restaurants I would ask the waiter if the chef would cut it up in the kitchen, which they were always happy to do. This allowed me to keep my dignity and eat my food as presented as opposed to having my food cut like a child's would be in front of others.

My left hand soon deteriorated until it was no longer able to bring fork to mouth. I had to be fed by my helpers. My request would be, "Feed me like a baby, but don't treat me like one." Eventually, even chewing and swallowing became more difficult.

I was also having trouble swallowing all my vitamins, minerals, herbs, and supplements as well as some prescription drugs. I could barely get it all down. Some were really gross-tasting despite being blended with chocolate milk. I dreaded it every night.

So in March 2013, it was time for a feeding tube. The way I looked at it, a feeding tube is a natural progression. It's another tool. It would allow me to continue to have a meaningful and even healthier life. Plus it didn't feel artificial. It was just another way to consume food. It might be silly, but I rationalized my decisions by thinking, "Could I survive on a desert island?" If the power went out, my food could be pulverized by hand, mixed with water then consumed through the tube.

But with a ventilator, desert island survival would be impossible. It's mechanical and isolating, and you become even more dependent. It would be like going from a cell phone back to a wall-mounted, corded phone. It's not natural, and for me, the quality of life one would have on a vent is questionable. Bottom line, I decided I don't want to be plugged in. But I was okay with getting my organ pierced, because that was hard-core.

It is important to get a feeding tube while one's breathing is still strong enough. This is measured by the FEV test (Forced Expiratory Volume). The doctors won't do surgery if one's breathing is below a certain number. So once I made the decision, I moved quickly.

My mom was really against me getting a feeding tube. The thought of it was really scary to her because Anne Marie passed away soon after receiving hers. My mom associated getting a feeding tube with imminent death.

Afterward she admitted, "It obviously turned out to be a

brilliant move. Definitely one of the times I'm glad Jenni did not listen to me and trusted her instinct."

I call my feeding tube "Canal Bistro," a play on a local cafe by the same name and my surgeon whose name was Dr. Canal. But since Philip was barely five at the time, we called it my "straw" in front of him. He understood that better.

In the beginning, for the first year and a half, I only used it to take my gross-tasting medicines and a morning protein shake. "Breakfast in bed!" It was easier for Jeff to get food into me on busy mornings. Sometimes I was barely awake.

The following summer, 2013, my in-laws took the whole family to Walt Disney World. I thought it would be a good idea to use my feeding tube on the trip for ease and convenience since eating by mouth took so long. It would be the first time I tried out my tube for meals other than my morning shake.

It was a hot June weekend when our group descended on Walt Disney World and the crowds were naturally whopping. Just sitting in my wheelchair, not moving at all, I was dripping with sweat. We found some relief on an air-conditioned boat ride through the *Little Mermaid Under the Sea* exhibit. As an unexpected perk, the family got a "princess pass"; wheelchair patrons and their families can bypass the lines of certain rides and enter through the exit. It goes without saying, there are advantages to traveling with "royalty."

Around noon, we all headed over to a busy hamburger joint for lunch. As everyone else settled at a table, my mom, Jeff, and I found a quiet corner, away from the crowds and the ragtime piano player, to feed me. We had brought pouches of Liquid Hope, one of the better liquified food products made for tube feedings. My mom had thoughtfully packed them in a cooler to keep them fresh in the heat. This turned out to be a not so great idea. Once she opened the pouch and tried to squeeze the food into my tube, we realized the problem. The contents had congealed in the cooler and it wouldn't pour out.

Jeff called the company who made the product for some advice and was told, a little too late, never to refrigerate the food because it will solidify. They also advised using a 60 cc syringe to push it in. But my doctors had advised against using a syringe for pushing food into my stomach because they said it was too fast of a method. The *doctor*-recommended formula was gravity-fed or poured into the tube. This "food" was a thin, watery liquid that, on paper, had the optimal amount of protein, vitamins, minerals, and calories, but, in fact, lacked real food. Basically it was chemicals and sugar, not what a Naturopath would order.

My mom and Jeff tried and tried to get Liquid Hope into my tube that day, even adding water to it and kneading it to soften it, but they finally gave up realizing the product was hopelessly solid. Instead, I ate a Mickey burger.

We would eventually get the hang of the feeding tube and acquire a knack for concocting wholesome, feeding-tube-friendly foods, but it would be months after the Disney trip before we revisited it. For the time being, I continued eating by mouth even though it was getting harder and more painstaking. Just a few bites would wear me out. Often I would eat something only to choke on it. Luckily I still had enough strength to cough it up. But even that was waning.

Consequently, I lost my appetite and more weight. By early 2014, I was becoming rail thin, malnourished and dehydrated. But I still wasn't ready to give up eating food by mouth.

One evening in the fall of 2014, a little scallion would change my life forever.

My mom heard the screaming siren first. It was some distance away . . . until it wasn't. She lived on a busier street, so sirens did not alarm her. I lived only a block away and my mom could see my house from the end of her driveway. But this night, as she casually stepped outside to get her mail, she saw that this time the flashing lights were at my house. Terrified, she tore down the street.

"How did you know? I purposely didn't call you because I didn't want you to worry," Jeff said when she flew through the front door. "I heard the siren! I saw the lights! I live right down the street!!"

The paramedics were leaning over me shining a small light down my throat while Jeff explained to my mom, "Philip's over at a friend's and we had planned a quiet evening. Jenni was craving Singapore noodles so we got carry-out Chinese and after just a couple of bites something didn't feel right. She has something stuck in her throat and can't get it up or down."

I knew I could aspirate this morsel of food any second. And I wasn't able to cough strongly enough to move it. I went into a full-blown panic attack. It went from bad to worse. I lost control of my bowels before I could get to the bathroom; I couldn't catch my breath; I was shaking; I was cold then hot, gagging, and dry heaving. That's when Jeff called 911.

The paramedics couldn't locate the food in my throat and the only thing they could suggest was to take me to the hospital and snake a scope down my throat. But since I was breathing and conscious and the procedure would be invasive, they didn't recommend it. Since there was nothing more that could be done, they left.

I knew I had to get the panic attack under control. I managed to keep it together enough to ask Jeff to call his sister-in-law Kim, who was an internist. He asked her to call in a prescription for anxiety medication. My mom was desperate to help her suffering daughter and ran to CVS to pick up the prescription. Meanwhile, Jeff put me to bed, tucking me into a comforting fetal position, and when my mom returned, he administered Ativan through my tube.

I was still trembling when my mom crawled into bed next to me and asked if she could try Matrix Energetics on me. I nodded. Pressing her hands tightly around my head, she visualized whatever was in my throat materializing in her throat and kept visualizing this until she actually felt something in her throat. That's when I began to relax and soon I felt it dislodge. Once freed, I was able to swallow it.

My mom had been trained in Matrix Energetics®, an alternative energy healing technique developed by a chiropractor/naturopathic physician. That night she was especially thankful that she had. The combination of the medication and my mother's love and energy finally melted away the panic.

My anxiety was under control. However, the inevitable was now here thanks to a wicked scallion that had gotten stuck onto the side of my esophagus like a piece of lettuce stuck to a salad bowl. I knew what was coming next. This horrific evening demonstrated that my swallowing muscles were failing, and it was becoming extremely dangerous to continue eating by mouth. For a brief time after the event, I tried to eat food, but I specified "nothing with an edge." This period was short-lived, and I soon found that my meals would have to be solely through my Canal Bistro.

Life was being reshuffled again and this time the cards were hurled all across the room. As another new normal emerged, my focus shifted to creating healthy, feeding-tube appropriate meals as well as recreating my clothing.

"Sodium selenate, phytonadione, molybdate," reading the ingredients on the pouch of Fibersource HN that the doctors handed me, I was disillusioned, to say the least. "These foods will keep you satisfied and they contain all the FDA-required nutrients," they told me.

But I knew better. I knew I could survive on this "food," but

I would never thrive on its chemically derived nutrition. The way my health had plummeted, I had to step up my game.

They knew tubes, but I knew nutrition. I studied it in med school. I took classes in food as medicine.

So as the doctors prattled on, trying to pitch their shiny foil packets of "high-nitrogen tube feeding formula," I said to myself, "Not gonna happen."

Just as I handled the effects of this disease from the early days, I turned eating through a tube on its head and came up with my own rules.

Partly inspired by Jason Becker's story, in which he made up his own recipes, plus my extensive background in holistic healing, I began MacGyvering my own formulas and was soon creating healthy meals using fresh, organic ingredients. I have streamlined the process over the years so all the ingredients are prepared ahead, frozen and ready for the Vitamix blender. We use syringes to get the food into the tube and have never had any problems with them, contrary to what the doctors had warned. When traveling or on the go, I use quality packaged foods like Liquid Hope and Orgain, an organic, healthy shake one might compare to Ensure.

Of course I miss eating! When I am at a table surrounded by food and people joyously eating and my belly is empty, it feels like the color is draining out of the room. I succumb to the inevitable pity and grief. In contrast, I can circumvent the feeling of deprivation if I don't allow myself to get too hungry. I make sure I eat before others eat. That way I can enjoy the smells and the appetizing look of the food without feeling sorry for myself.

As my disease progresses, my stomach and calorie requirements continue to shrink. I've discovered that smaller, more frequent meals are required to keep my belly full, blood sugar stable, and my world a happier, satiated place.

Using my Canal Bistro to consume my homemade meals, my relative health has been restored. I put on weight and color returned to my cheeks. Once again I looked the epitome of health, except of course for that pesky ALS.

My Grandma Ruth, said, in her not-so-subtle way, "You look so good! What are you doing?"

"I'm eating."

"That's it? I can't believe that's it. You looked so awful before!"

Gotta love grandmas!

Having food injected in a tube inserted into your stomach presents a particular problem—modesty. When this new eating regimen began, it was fall going into winter, and a shirt or sweater over a pair of jeans or leggings was easy to work around. But when summer came, and with it sundresses, mealtime became showtime at the Berebitskys. I had long since dispensed with underwear (one fewer thing to have to worry about pulling up and down while also eliminating those irksome wedgies), so if I wanted food, I had to go for the Full Monty.

It never really came to that, but it did present a challenge until I came up with a solution, and one of my helpers introduced me to Sharon, a great seamstress.

I asked Sharon if she could cut slits in all my dresses near where the feeding tube would be. Then I came up with the idea for her to fashion a flap over the slit to cover the opening, a "Peek-a-tube." Sharon's workshop was filled with colorful and whimsical fabrics that happened to pair nicely with my assortment of sundresses. Voila! Easy and yet demure access! And the new flaps added a unique flair. She continues to alter my dresses this way, including more formal ones.

Speaking of my feeding tube, it was time to make another change. At this point, my G-tube was a silicone tube that extended 12 inches out from the opening of my stomach. I had to figure out what to do with this long thing when not in use. I tried stuffing it in my bra or in a pocket with limited success. Also, there's no good way to clean it since it is always attached to me. Cola drinkers may cringe to know that pouring Coca-Cola® through the tube is the recommended way to unclog it, my personal Drano®. I wish I had asked the doctor if Pepsi® would do the same—my own Pepsi Challenge.

Though I continually questioned my doctor about why I had to have a G-tube, a tube permanently attached to one's body, as opposed to the G-button that could make life easier, it took me a year to realize I was not going to change his mind. The reality, once again: it's my body and I need to take matters into my own hands.

The G-button, a device that fits into the surgical opening made in the stomach, acts as a portal for the temporary insertion of a 12-inch tube. When not in use, the tube can be unhooked from the portal and the button closed. The benefit of the button is that it is small and compact and fits close against the abdomen so it doesn't get in the way. The unhooked tube can then be more thoroughly cleaned. But most gastroenterologists generally only use buttons in children; adults must deal with the long, cumbersome G-tube.

I watched a YouTube video on how to switch out the tube for the button and talked with several doctors until I finally found one who was willing to do the procedure.

The end result was wonderful but not without some drama/trauma. Removing the tube was a little barbaric. The doctor braced one of his hands on my shoulder and with the other pulled the tube with all his might. Imagine a half-dollar size silicon washer needing to come through a hole the size of a dime.

He was pulling with such force that when it finally came out I expected the doctor to be flung across the room. That didn't happen, but blood did splash all over Jeff's glasses. We made it! I was finally free of my fifth appendage and now, years later, I continue to have complete success with the button.

NOTE: *I need to have the button changed about every three to four months, but this procedure is a piece-of-cake.*

My gut had led me in the right direction . . . pun intended.

CHAPTER 8: Decisions, Decisions, So Many Decisions

When eating by mouth was no longer an option, it was time for a feeding tube.

Jeff feeding Jenni
(5 years, 5 months after diagnosis)
Photography: IndyStar/USA Today Network

Dinner is served. Combination of shredded chicken (previously frozen into single serving pouches), organic greens, & sunflower seed butter; to get the consistency needed, blended twice in a *Vitamix Personal Blender*

MIC-KEY® Low Profile Gastrostomy Feeding Tube (G-button) & insertion of removable feeding tube

Artfully designed "peek-a-tubes" by Sharon McKittrick

Photography by
Conrad Piccirillo
& Lisa Boncosky

CHAPTER 9
Have Wheelchair Will Travel

"What's up, girl?"

"Stay strong, sister."

"Hey baby, you better slow down or I'll have to write you a ticket."

"You hungry? I'm hungry, too. I haven't eaten in two days."

As I rolled by, people living on the streets of San Francisco's Mission District called out to me. I've also heard similar shout-outs while visiting Chicago and other cities.

There's something about being in a wheelchair that connects you with people who have hardships of their own. It's an instant bond, a family tie. You can see my struggle: it's there, right out in the open, just as it is for a person who is homeless. There's no masking the suffering. And no one ever asks me for money or blames me for their misfortune.

Only once, in downtown Indy, did the opposite happen. A passerby, while watching Jeff fuss over putting on my sunglasses, offered to help. We told him, "No thank you, we're fine."

Refusing to take no for an answer, he said, "No, I insist, let me help."

Then he tossed a dollar bill in my lap! We chuckled about the irony as he strutted away, apparently satisfied with his good deed. Two thoughts ran through my head: my faith in humanity was elevated, and my wardrobe needs an upgrade.

In the spring of 2014, Jeff and I traveled to Colorado and

California for two back-to-back weddings. Between the two weddings, we took a side-trip to El Cerrito, California, to see our friends, Karen and Alex, at their spectacular cliffside home. The cliffside was no obstacle. Alex and Karen simply carried me in my push wheelchair up and down the steep steps leading to the front door. My heavy Permobil stayed in the van. It was a fun, carefree few days with friends and I remember it all fondly.

The most significant part of the trip was the last leg: the wedding of my brother, Rob, and his fiancé Gerri, in Sonoma, California. We stayed in nearby Santa Rosa, the home of the Charles M. Shultz Museum, which was full of Snoopys, Lucys, and Charlie Browns.

I officiated the wedding, a true honor and distinction. When Rob first asked me to officiate, I said "No way. I don't like the way I sound, the way I speak. I'm going to be too nervous. What if I'm not well enough? I don't want to mess up your wedding." He asked me to please, please just promise to think about it.

I did just that. I felt honored to be asked and wanted to embrace this opportunity. Fear was not going to get in my way. Once I had a moment to think it through, I knew that if Jeff stood beside me, as a team we could do this! The official and "touchy/feely parts" would be mine, and he would fill in the rest.

For eight bucks I got my online certificate and prepared for what was to be an extraordinary ceremony. Thanks to a creative audio guy and an awesome mic, all went well, and the 100-plus guests could all hear me perfectly. I chose sand to symbolize the marriage union. Rob and Gerri poured their individual vials of sand into one, marking their solemn and inseparable bond. All the while the air was perfumed with the fragrance of orchids from leis flown in from Hawaii, Gerri's home, and draped around the bridal party's necks.

It was a wonderful time—so much fun and so, so special.

With all the excitement, however, I had to pee all the time. Every other minute Jeff had to take me to the bathroom.

"With all that was going on, we basically had to just give up on Philip, as we were so busy with each other and the ceremony," Jeff added. "We gave him free rein. He probably drank eight glasses of root beer that night."

One of the highlights for Philip was finding a cute, little stray dog that he befriended.

Officiating at Rob and Gerri's wedding will remain one of my favorite memories.

I had to get past my initial "can't do" to be there for their "I do." I reframed my thinking into my newer mantras, "Live in the present" and "You are not really living if you don't have a little fear to overcome." I tried to extract every drop of living out of this occasion. Officiating at the ceremony made me feel fabulous. I stepped over my fear, embraced the full experience, and connected with the love and happiness of the day.

The take-away is that no one is guaranteed anything more than this moment, but few realize it. My condition has cleared my path of pettiness and opened my eyes to live in the present. It may not always be happy or pretty, but it is what I have. I have learned to be intentional in how I spend my time. And by doing this I am able to find joy and humor in what life has given me.

The wedding also marked the end of the family feud that had begun eight years earlier at my wedding. We were wary at first, thinking it might be awkward having all of us together again. To our delight, everyone got along and the past was finally laid to rest. Everyone was gracious and kind to one another.

Six-year-old Philip, swimming in root beer, was thrilled to meet my half-brothers, his uncles, who were in their pre- and early teens. He had trouble understanding that they were his uncles. To him they were either his brothers or cousins. Uncles were much older. But no matter, he loved them and I was thrilled they were now in each others' lives.

We had come full circle as a family and there was a big "smiley face" inside.

As fabulous as our travelogue sounds, it's important to dig a little deeper and note what goes on in order for us to travel at all. See Appendix B for our Travel List.

We only take trips that meet our standard of what's travel-worthy. Not all trips are worth the time, effort, and expense.

We call ahead with our needs and the local ALS Association arranges to have the items ready for our arrival.

After the Colorado/California trip, we had to make a checklist of all these things because we left something in every city we went to. And you can't exactly go to CVS and pick up another mouthpiece for an air machine.

For air travel, we always take two carry-on bags: one containing the Trilogy air machine*, chargers and batteries, and one containing everything I need for my feeding tube. We never put these essentials in checked luggage.

*Non-invasive Ventilator. NIPPV, also known as Bilevel Positive Airway Pressure (Bi-Pap) is an electronic breathing device.

It's been our experience that Southwest Airlines has been the most accommodating and well-equipped to handle a wheelchair and my various needs. While other airlines have their baggage handlers manually lift my 400-pound wheelchair, Southwest terminals are equipped with dollies to lift the chair into the luggage compartment of the airplane. One time, when traveling on another airlines, we watched from the window as two, then three and eventually four big guys struggled to lift my chair onto the conveyor belt and finally into the plane.

It's customary for those in a wheelchair to board the plane first and get off last. In our case, before we can get off we have to wait for my wheelchair to be retrieved from the baggage compartment and brought down the gangway to the plane door. The entire staff has to wait along with us. Once again, our experience with Southwest has been that their staff wait happily and patiently.

Then there are the people who have to transfer me: from my wheelchair to the aisle wheelchair (a very skinny chair on wheels that fits down the aisle of the plane) to my seat and then the reverse order once we land. At the Indianapolis Airport, there is a Southwest Airlines employee named Stretch who can lift me with his pinkie. And he remembers us every time.

Once at our destination, we have to have a wheelchair-accessible hotel room as well as a wheelchair-accessible rental van or cab.

NOTE: *Confirm your hotel room. Handicap accessible does not always mean wheelchair accessible. Occasionally we have gotten a room that has bars in the bathroom (a.k.a handicap accessible) but no space for my wheelchair to turn around in the sleeping area. We (and by "we" I mean Jeff) have even had to rearrange the hotel furniture to get me in and out.*

Going back to Southwest Airlines, here's a particular example of extraordinary service onboard a Southwest flight where I joined a different kind of "Mile High Club." It was horrendous, the stuff nightmares are made of, but the flight attendant and, as always, Jeff were beyond amazing.

FYI: For those concerned parents, during the following episode our thoughts were not on Philip. But when we finally returned to our seats we were thrilled to discover Philip was completely engrossed in a movie on his iPad and was unaware of our extended absence.

It started off simply enough. While in flight I needed to use the restroom. FYI: #1. The trouble began when we discovered there was no aisle-wheelchair onboard. So Jeff and the flight attendant, who had previously offered to help in any way she could, had to carry me to the bathroom. Even though this single-person-sized bathroom was extremely cramped, awkward, and tricky, the three of us squeezed in and managed to pull my pants down, place me on the toilet and offer me some semblance of privacy. Mission accomplished? No, the story doesn't end there.

They now had to get me off the toilet and pull up my pants. Before the bathroom break, I had gotten very cold, so I had several scarves wrapped around me. As Jeff lifted me up, Jen, the flight attendant, reached her arms around Jeff to pull up my pants. Little did they both realize that this maneuver was bunching my many layers of scarves and strangling me. I was literally unable to breathe. Shear panic engulfed me but no words could come out of my breathless mouth. "Is this really it? Headline will read: ALS patient outlived her prognosis but dies from unintentional strangulation in airplane restroom."

After finally getting my pants pulled up, they sat me back on the toilet to figure out how to carry me back to my seat. Wait! What happens when someone's oxygen is being cut off? They poop. Even though I was finally able to take a breath, my body still did the natural oxygen-deprived reflex. Oh shit! Literally. I now had a full load in my pants.

Jeff was on his knees in the teeny, tiny airplane bathroom painstakingly cleaning me up. After what seemed like an eternity, I had a clean but very naked bottom and an unwearable pair of pants. Jen again came to the rescue. She reached her hand through the door and offered Jeff a pair of her workout leggings. When I was once again fully clothed, my knight and knightess in shining armor carried me back to my seat. Jen's graciousness and generosity soothed the mounting embarrassment I was experiencing. Thank you Jen and thank you Southwest for hiring such kind-hearted people.

Now back to our travel adventures.

On a recent trip to New York where we went purely for fun and entertainment with our good friends Lisa (a.k.a my "Cruise Director") and her husband Bill, we discovered that the cabs that are accessible don't always have seat belts. I have to be belted to the seat or I will fall over. This was an ongoing dilemma during our stay.

Another unexpected obstacle was that not all subway stops were wheelchair accessible. We found this out the hard way when trying to get to the 9/11 Memorial. We were able to get on the subway but getting off was the problem. The closest accessible subway stop that had a way to get a wheelchair back to street level was still two miles from our desired destination. Unfortunately we never made it to the Memorial. Instead we got to enjoy Greenwich Village. Once again, life kept giving us opportunities to learn how to roll with the punches.

Despite the difficulties we encountered, in general we find that everywhere we go most people go out of their way to help us. We love having the chance to see the humanity in people.

CHAPTER 9: Have Wheelchair Will Travel

Gerri, Rob, Jeff, Mickey Mouse,
Philip, Joyce & Jenni
(3 years, 7 months after diagnosis)

Walt Disney World®

Berebitsky/Asher family
(4 years, 3 months
after diagnosis)

Jenni enjoying Butter Beer

**The Wizarding World of Harry
Potter™ at Universal Florida™**

(3 years, 7 months after diagnosis)

Jenni, Joyce, Rob & Gerri
Outside of *Hogwarts School of
Witchcraft and Wizardry*

CHAPTER 9: Have Wheelchair Will Travel

Jenni & *Troll Under the Bridge*

Seattle, WA
(4 years,
4 months
after diagnosis)

Tessa & Jenni, day before
Tessa & Mike's wedding

Jenni with
Naturopathic
friends: Kate,
Amy, Alena
& Natasha

Jenni officiating Gerri & Rob's Wedding
5/9/14
Santa Rosa, CA
(5 years, 2 months
after diagnosis)

With siblings & cousins day
after the wedding

Jeff, Philip & Jenni in
Snoopy's hometown

CHAPTER 9: Have Wheelchair Will Travel

Jeff, Jenni, Lisa & Bill
on Broadway
New York, New York
(7 years, 2 months
after diagnosis)

With family, San Jose, CA
(6 years, 5 months after diagnosis)

Jenni & Philip
Washington, DC
(4 years, 7 months
after diagnosis)

Joyce & Jenni,
La Jolla, CA
(4 years, 11 months
after diagnosis)

Jeff, Jenni, Joyce & Philip seeing *Hamilton: An American Musical*
& visiting friends: Rosensteins & Andreadises
Chicago, IL (8 years, 4 months after diagnosis)

CHAPTER 10

All My People Showed Up

In the spring of 2014, Jeff's brother-in-law David said, "Hey Jeff. How about doing this year's Indianapolis Sprint Triathlon with me?"

To which Jeff replied, "Are you crazy, David? I don't have time for that. I've got responsibilities. I'd have to take Jenni with me."

My ears perked up and I chimed in, "Don't tease me, I'd love to do that!"

And a great idea was born.

Over the next several weeks, we strategized on how we could become a team with me as the central participant. A lifelong swimmer, Jeff was a natural for the swim. My cousin Mark, an experienced cyclist and Ironman, handled the bike portion, and my Ironman brother, Rob, was a "shoe-in" as my runner for the final leg of the race.

Jeff tied a tow belt around his waist with a cord that attached to a rubber raft. Lisa, my human seat belt, and I sat in the raft. She was there to make sure I stayed upright. Jeff would then swim the 500-meter course in Eagle Creek Reservoir, towing us behind him. Mark would ride the wheelchair bike with me strapped in throughout the 10-mile bike course, and Rob would push me in the same wheelchair for the three-mile run.

Individually we each trained for our specific event. How did I train? I had to be prepared to sit in any situation. As a team, we practiced transitions using my "flying carpet." We got me from my power wheelchair into the raft; out of the raft into the specialized wheelchair that was clipped onto the bike; and last, unclipped the wheelchair from the bike for the run.

Jeff contacted Team Hoyt, a father and son team who have competed in triathlons, duathlons and half and full marathons for over 35 years. In 1962, oxygen deprived at birth, Rick was born with cerebral palsy and quadriplegia. In 1977, he told his dad he wanted to participate in a benefit run for a friend who had been paralyzed in an accident. That was the first of over 1,100 races for the two-man team, including running and biking 3,735 miles across the United States in 45 days. In the spring of 2014, they ran their 32nd and last Boston Marathon together, Dick at age 74 and Rick at age 52. They were helpful and encouraging to Jeff and steered him to the proper tow belts and rafts for our endeavor.

August 16, 2014, arrived rainy and cool with temperatures only reaching 50 degrees, but the athletes were ripped and ready for the showdown at Eagle Creek Park. The race was to begin at 8:00 AM with participants arriving around 6:00 AM. When our alarm clock trilled at 4:30 AM, we hit the ground running.

As soon as we arrived at the park, we were greeted by a local morning show TV reporter and a photographer from the *Indianapolis Star*. The sun wasn't even up yet and my team and I were being interviewed, filmed and photographed. Sharing my adventure with Indy added to the excitement of the day.

Our team was ready to begin the swimming event when a voice came over the loudspeakers announcing, "Everyone come down to the beach as The J Team prepares to launch." The theme song from *Rocky III*, "Eye of the Tiger," was played, pumping up the crowd. Five hundred people gathered at the beach to watch Jeff swim the course with Lisa and me tethered to him by the tow belt. Everyone cheered us on. It was the first time the Indianapolis Sprint Triathlon had a raft rider in the race.

It was transcendental. I have never felt so uplifted by so many people—spiritually and emotionally. My friends and family all wore J-Team t-shirts in brown and yellow, replicating the colors in the sunflower that we had chosen as our symbol.

Ann Tudor, a glass artist and friend of my mom's, made sunflower necklaces, which we called JenFlowers, for our supporters (proceeds going to the local ALS Association). To add to the festivities, my mom painted sunflowers on the faces of the eager cheerleaders.

The swim part was great since I had Lisa in the raft to keep me warm and entertained. The biking and running went well, except I had no jacket and felt the brunt of the bitter wind and rain. Unprepared for the weather, the only towels we had were already wet from the swim. After the race was completed, a kind soul saw us desperately trying to warm me and offered a blanket from the first-aid tent.

Afterward, there was a party at our house. Once home, however, I hit the wall. I was hungry. I hadn't eaten since my breakfast shake. I was exhausted, and I was still cold to the bone. People were hugging and touching me constantly and suddenly I needed to get away from it all. I quietly fled to my bedroom and into my closet to cry. After a few tears, a little quiet time and a much needed meal of Liquid Hope, I felt better and could rejoin the party.

The triathlon was such a high and was so amazing that when it was over, I crashed. But afterwards, when I thought about it, I actually relished my discomfort. Athletes suffer, so why shouldn't I experience the exhilaration of all aspects of a triathlon, something I'd longed to do since Rob had first competed in the Ironman. I had the thrill of victory and the agony . . . without the defeat. I was first in my division! I probably should mention that I was the only one in that division.

I jokingly call the triathlon and the ALS Walk, which was a few weeks later, my High Holidays. In the Jewish faith, everyone shows up at Temple for these holidays. For me, "All my people showed up."

Once I rejoined the party in my backyard, I watched as Ice

Bucket Challenges were recorded and sent out by various people, including one that Philip sent to his school. His challenge was accepted and Philip became a hero. And in the eyes of Philip and his classmates, I also became a hero.

That year the Ice Bucket Challenge, a fundraiser for ALS research, was a viral phenomenon, even reaching the President of the United States. To everyone's amazement, it raised hundreds of millions of dollars. The money was and is being spent diligently on genetic research, biomarker identification, clinical trials, drug development, and education as well as on patient and community services. For me, the recognition and acknowledgement of what I have been dealing with helped make me feel connected and understood. It also made it a lot easier to explain to people why I'm in a wheelchair.

Once my triathlon story aired on television and was printed in the paper, the Berebitskys were known around town. At the ice cream parlor a few weeks after the competition, Jeff and Philip had Piper with them and some people were admiring the sweet dog.

"That's my mom's service dog," said seven-year-old Philip. "My mom has ALS."

"Oh! I read about her in the paper," they said. "I know who she is!"

Philip came home and told me, "Mom, I wish you didn't have ALS, but at least we're famous."

When the Sprint Triathlon came around the next year I was excited to be able to participate again. I had learned my lesson the hard way in the previous year's event, so I came prepared for any weather. Fortunately, August 15, 2015, was a beautiful, dry, 70-degree day. This time, I was properly fed and hydrated. This time, I paced myself so I didn't get overwhelmed and tired.

Jeff repeated his swim with Lisa reprising her role as my human seat belt. The lake was beautiful, the ride was peaceful and dry! I only got one drop of water on me. This year there were a few substitutions. Alex, our friend from California, became the cyclist and our Rabbi, Brett, the runner. All my people, in their brown J-Team t-shirts, painted sunflower faces, and pom-poms, were there to cheer my team on. This year, the only suffering I experienced was that I needed to pee half way through the race. I chose not to be a true competitor (which would mean peeing on myself). Instead I was thankful for great bladder control.

CHAPTER 10: All My People Showed Up

Indianapolis Sprint Triathlon
8/16/14
The J Team
Jeff, Rob, Lisa, Mark & Jenni
(5 years, 5 months after diagnosis)

CHAPTER 10: All My People Showed Up

Indianapolis Sprint Triathlon
8/15/15
The J Team
Jeff, Alex, Rabbi Brett, Jenni & Lisa
(6 years, 5 months after diagnosis)

CHAPTER 10: All My People Showed Up

Interviews by local TV stations

1st Indianapolis Sprint Triathlon
(5 years, 5 months after diagnosis)

2nd ALS Ice Bucket Challenge
(6 years, 5 months after diagnosis)

ALS Ice Bucket Challenge

CHAPTER 11
The Importance of Moving

The motion of my life has become a paradox, moving in fast-forward while stuck in pause at the same time. Life events and planning for them seem to move along rapidly. Yet my day-to-day experiences feel like a giant pause button has been pushed. Immobility is beyond frustrating; however, I have found the gift. I feel akin to Shel Silverstein's book, *The Missing Piece.* I see things that a body in motion would miss. I experience life with a heightened sense of awareness.

But don't get me wrong, gift or not, ALS sucks.

I was a fit, health-conscious, vibrant young woman until, without warning and for no reason, I was stricken with a hideous disease that is slowly paralyzing every voluntary muscle in my body. What remains now, in 2017, is partial movement of my left hand, diaphragm, and speech muscles. By some miracle, my smile muscles remain completely unaffected.

I used to be athletic. I loved to swim, hike, run, and bike. I enjoyed being a bike commuter in Portland as well as climbing the steps of Mt. Tabor. I relished being able to push myself to do more. I practiced yoga and GYROTONIC® regularly.

Now I can't eat, hug, wave, dress, hold a book, sit up, stand up, stir soup, use the bathroom alone, put on lipstick, wipe my tears, scratch an itch, blow my nose, tickle my son or even reach out to hold my husband's hand. I can hardly remember what it's like to do those things anymore. Speaking is hard. Breathing is hard.

And yet, I have not given up on my body, even though my body continues to give up on me.

In 2007, I became a GYROTONIC® instructor in Portland,

Oregon. The fundamentals of the GYROTONIC EXPANSION SYSTEM® consist of a new exercise technique using GYROKINESIS® principles, which are movements that focus on the spiraling and undulations of the body and spine while opening the joints. It is an experience unlike any other type of conditioning regime. GYROTONIC® training moves the work onto specialized equipment including the Gyrotonic Pulley Tower.

I developed a real love for this form of exercise. In 2010, when we arrived in Indy, I searched for a local gyro instructor. I found a perfect match with Katie at Pilates Indy Inc. As my needs changed, Katie responded and adapted. Katie learned how to be my arms and legs, allowing me to continue to get the full benefit of the gyro exercises.

We had to get creative with transfers when Katie became pregnant. I sought the help of my friend Mickie, an occupational therapist. She taught us how to use a slide board which, by the way, was borrowed from the ALS loan closet. The slide board has been renamed "The Jenni Mover" and has become an irreplaceable tool at the studio.

The early part of ALS comes with a lot of spasms and cramping. I found deep muscle massages to be very helpful in relieving these discomforts. I turned to Donna, a friend and massage therapist, trained in the Pfrimmer technique. First I started having massages once a month; as my disease progressed, so did the frequency. Eventually I needed a weekly massage to remain as comfortable as possible.

Donna's massage studio was on the second floor, so when I could no longer climb the stairs, we had to become creative. We borrowed another studio that was accessible. Eventually it made more sense for me to purchase a massage table and for Donna to come to my house. Not only does she give me a massage, she has fun adding her special touches as she gets me ready for the day. Having similar tastes, she has become one of my favorite clothing

shoppers, scouring resale shops for the perfect "Jenni outfits."
For all these reasons, I look forward to my Monday morning
"ahhhhh."

The final addition to my exercise regime was physical
therapy. Once a week, Barb, at Rehabilitation Hospital of
Indiana, offers a variety of therapies from ultrasound to much
needed stretches, twists, and pulls to keep my over-cooked-limp-
noodle body as comfortable as possible.

I have been able to fill my week with what I call my
exercise routine: massage and physical therapy once a week and
gyro twice a week. I am committed to being as physically active
as possible, even if I'm not the one doing the heavy lifting. I do
all of these activities without pushing myself to the point of
muscle loss like I did so many summers before. I believe that
these activities are the reason I am relatively pain-free.
Unfortunately none of these exercises can totally eliminate my
sore tush.

CHAPTER 11: The Importance of Moving

Jenni hiking Hawaii (4 months after diagnosis)

Jenni, age 26, Melbourne, Australia

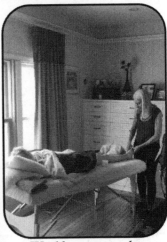

Weekly massages by Donna Dorman (8 years, 8 months after diagnosis)

Twice weekly GYROTONIC® - Pilates Indy Inc. (2 years, 4 months after diagnosis)

Weekly Physical Therapy - Rehabilitation Hospital of Indiana (8 years, 10 months after diagnosis)

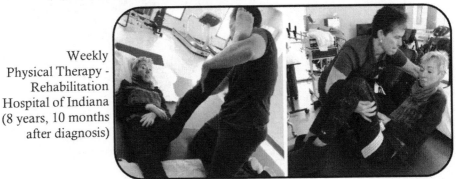

CHAPTER 12
Hands-Free Parenting

Speaking of moving and pain-in-the-tushes, we have Philip. Those of you who have children will understand. Although he is high energy, a force to be reckoned with, and a body in constant motion, I would not trade him for anything in the world. With his spirit and zest for life comes a fun-loving and very empathic young man.

Philip came into this world with an intensity and passion that was present from the moment he popped his head out. It's like he knew he would be an only child born into a family with unique circumstances and needs.

Raising Philip (and we are not done yet!) has had its challenges (as does raising any child) but anyone who meets him knows there is something really special about him. His vivaciousness and charisma are contagious. These are skills that have been and will always be a gift to him as he navigates our family's ever-changing dynamics.

Philip had to learn early that he would have to share his dad's attention not with a sibling but with a mother who continues to lose her physical abilities. Sadly, I remember when five-year-old Philip said to Jeff, "But, Dad, I need you, too."

Philip loves his cousins and friends, and he has many, yet he still grapples with the wish to have a sibling. Both Jeff and I would have loved to have had more children but that ain't happening. One more reality we have all had to accept.

When kids are young, much of their parents' power or authority comes from physical intervention, something I was losing rapidly. I had to figure out and negotiate my parental role: being in charge of a three-year-old who was stronger than I was. I had to accept that I would win some battles and lose others. I remember sitting on the floor of his bedroom trying to get him to take a nap. The only power I had was the weight of my entire body to prevent him from opening the door. I struggled to keep my position in place while he struggled to open the door. After what seemed like an eternity, he finally gave up and got into bed to take his nap.

Philip, like many children, would often crave physical affection: like hugging, squeezing, and kissing. This would be fine except that I had neither the ability to shower him with the affection I wanted to give him nor the physical ability to stop him when he went too far with me or others.

Being the recipient of Philip's occasional aggressive and inappropriate behavior left me in a quandary. An able-bodied parent could stop the behavior by steering the child away or holding back their hand or body. I was able to do none of that, so we sought counsel from a wonderful local parenting coach. I learned that my power lay in withholding my attention, which is really what most kids want. Even though I couldn't walk away or block him, I could turn my head and close my eyes, giving him the feedback that what he was doing was not acceptable. I was amazed how quickly this method worked. Philip soon learned what was okay and not okay.

When Philip was about five he went through a stage of putting his finger in his butt and smelling it. A typical but gross little kid thing to do. But he crossed the line when he wanted me to smell it as well. I couldn't do anything to stop his advancing finger. The next thing I knew his smelly finger was up my nostril. I felt disgusted, violated, and humiliated. Trying to hide my tears and the degree of upset from Philip, I groped for the controls of my wheelchair to escape the scene of the crime.

Philip followed me into my bedroom and saw that I was sobbing. He was devastated and burst into tears himself. It turned out my upset was actually the best lesson for him. There we were, mother and son, crying over a stinky finger. I was able to talk him through my emotional reaction, and, in turn, he learned a valuable lesson on a visceral level. He never, ever did anything like that again.

For several years during the beginning of my disease, I dreaded the idea that my ever-changing body's abilities, or lack thereof, would become a source of embarrassment for Philip. Then I had an epiphany: at some point every kid will find something mortifying about their parents. I could be the healthiest, hippest mom, and Philip would *still* be embarrassed about something. To be embarrassed by your parent is part of the circle of life. Accepting this as "normal" lifted a huge weight off my shoulders.

We have learned, like many other families, there are compromises we all have to make. For us, Philip's extracurricular activities have to be based on proximity and frequency. Jeff can only be spread so thin. At times this is frustrating, but we do our best to give Philip the extras that we know he most enjoys.

An interesting plus to our situation is that Philip is learning a lot about empathy and taking care of another's needs. Shortly after I got my new, not as easily maneuverable controls on my wheelchair, Philip, Jeff, and I were grocery shopping. At one point, Jeff left Philip and me to wander while he did the shopping more quickly on his own. I have a slim range of temperature tolerance. I often joke I have two degrees of comfort—73° to 74°. Sitting in my wheelchair with my winter coat on and new chin driving device wrapped around my neck, I began to get very hot, anxious, and claustrophobic.

I asked Philip to look for his dad. When Philip returned and said he couldn't find him, I panicked. I told him he had to find his dad. He looked me right in the eye and said, "Mom, can I help you?"

My silly nine-year-old transformed into a calm and confident caretaker.

Taking his lead, I was able to restore my calm and replied, "Yes. Please take my coat off."

Philip rose to my needs and carefully and efficiently removed my jacket. Just so you know, at this point I had no control of my arms. I was no help. Philip mirrored the exact steps Jeff uses to undress me. It made my heart sing to realize how observant Philip had been even when I had no idea he was paying attention.

When one's physical abilities are limited, it's not only the discipline side of parenting that's harder, it's also the loving and affection part, too. Philip can be lying right next to me and I can't touch him. These can be moments of pure torture. Sometimes when he is lying in bed next to me, I'll turn my head and stare at him. He'll turn and look at me.

"Mom, what?"

I tell him that my staring is my way of loving on him.

I remember one time my mom was in the bedroom with us. She was kidding around with Philip and I told her, "He has such a cute tush. Please squeeze it for me."

As he squealed and my mom laughed, I smiled while imagining it was my hands doing the squeezing. The lack of tickling, kissing, and basic physical forms of affection is missing for both of us. Unfortunately, I have no great words of wisdom for this. It's just another loss, another form of collateral damage from this disease.

A reporter once asked me, "How did the Ice Bucket Challenge affect you and your family?"

I answered, "The increased awareness of ALS made explaining to people why I am in a wheelchair easier."

With my publicity and recent fame from the triathlon and the Ice Bucket Challenge, Philip had begun to think of me as a rock star, not an invalid.

A highlight for Philip was when his school accepted his Ice Bucket Challenge. The entire school gathered outside to watch as two students chosen from each class dumped water on their respective teachers. All the students loved every minute of it. How ironic that my disease would make Philip a "King-for-the-day." For the first time, he comprehended what it meant that his mom has ALS.

From then on, the awkwardness that some of the students felt around me in my wheelchair was gone. The best part is that Philip finally got to see my disease as something other than "my mom has bendy hands." It also instilled in him a sense of pride and protectiveness for me. He began to feel as though he was a part of helping our family cope with our personal challenges as opposed to being an outsider looking in.

CHAPTER 12: Hands-Free Parenting
Jenni & Philip

Philip's 1st snow, 13 months old (3 months before diagnosis)

Philip, 15 months old Florida Keys (2 weeks before diagnosis)

Philip, 9 months old (7 months before diagnosis)

Philip, 13 months old La Jolla, CA (3 months before diagnosis)

Mommy & Me gym, Portland, OR (5 days after diagnosis)

Philip, age 2, Portland, OR (7 months after diagnosis)

CHAPTER 12: Hands-Free Parenting
Jenni & Philip

(2 years, 9 months after diagnosis)

(2 years after diagnosis)

Indianapolis Colts game (5 years, 7 months after diagnosis)

(3 years, 10 months after diagnosis)

(6 years, 10 months after diagnosis)

Joyce, Elliot & Afi (mom, dad & stepmom) with their furry babies (5 years, 8 months after diagnosis)

La Jolla, CA (7 years, 11 months after diagnosis)

CHAPTER 13
Unofficial Words of Wisdom

I highly recommend having a therapist. Someone who will care about you but won't be emotionally invested in what you say. Therapists and counselors are trained to keep a certain amount of objectivity.

Friends and family are irreplaceable, but in my experience, the desire to protect them may interfere with things you need to say. I was lucky to find someone I could completely open up to. These lessons or gems I learned from her have really made a difference for me:

Not my body, not my space
A mantra I use to help me separate my own issues and circumstances from other people's drama.

My tendency is to feel responsible. If someone is upset, I find myself racking my brain to try to come up with a way to fix it.

Example: I'm very close with my mom. When she is upset, I become emotionally entwined. I ask myself, did I do something to cause the upset? Can I do anything to change the situation and make it go away?

This mantra has helped me distinguish between feeling responsible for other people's upset and my desire to make things better. In reality, everyone is on their own journey, responsible for themselves. I can help, but I don't have to take on their emotions.

Is it true, is it kind, and is it necessary
I ask myself these questions when deciding whether to say something I feel compelled to share. What I've learned is not

everything needs to be communicated and expressed, at least not to the person it could upset.

Example: I'd like to give you an example, but the few I can think of would hurt the individuals' feelings when they read this book—thus it would not be kind or necessary to disclose it here.

Future negative fantasy

This is a form of daydreaming about all the doom and gloom to come. When we look into the future, we think we are seeing the truth but it's no more than our imaginations. When you focus on the doom and gloom, you experience the upset in the present and miss out on what is happening right now. We have no idea what the future may hold. Prognoses are based on statistics, not what will happen to you specifically.

Example: When I've been at bar and bat mitzvahs of friends and family, it was easy for me to start thinking of Philip's bar mitzvah, and how I won't be there. What will Jeff do? What will Philip do? Before I know it, I'd have tears in my eyes. The first time this happened Philip was four and now he is ten. I have to remind myself that I do *not* know what time frame I have.

Living in the upset now does not make the future different. It just makes the present yucky. This is one of the harder concepts to grasp but one of the most productive and helpful. I don't want to mislead you into thinking that what I'm saying is that I'm perfect at living each day to the fullest, because I'm not. I'm just committed to living my life as true to myself as possible.

Balcony vs basement people

It's important to surround ourselves with people who bring us up in life, as opposed to those who bring us down. Those who bring us down could be loved ones. You can't necessarily remove them from your life, but it's important to create boundaries to protect yourself from their "basement" thinking.

Know where your guilt comes from

We all have a set of rules for the different roles we play, i.e., daughter/son, mom/dad, wife/husband, friend, etc. These rules are created by our history and our collective environment. We think these rules are how things have to be. So when we deviate, we compensate by feeling guilty. By realizing that these rules are arbitrary and made up we can alleviate some of the guilt we may be feeling.

Example: My mom believes that being a good mom means that she should know my needs without me asking. So when she doesn't do what I need intuitively, she feels guilty. This guilt makes her beat herself up and feel bad, which doesn't serve either one of us. It was a big "aha" for her when we uncovered this gem. Eliminating guilt opens doors to communication and allows us to be more present in the moment. My mom came to this realization only as we were writing this book.

Hospice might be the right choice

Choosing hospice doesn't mean you're dying tomorrow. For many the thought of hospice is off limits. It's as if talking about it is wishing for someone to die. This is an old-fashioned view of something that can be helpful. I have to admit I was no different than the norm. Even though I had been eligible for hospice care for about a year before I decided to use it, I kept it at a distance. It had an ominous feeling. It was a taboo subject. When my doctors would bring it up, I would shut it down. I thought once I acknowledged hospice, I was accepting defeat. I couldn't have been more wrong.

Years earlier, my mom had had a positive experience with hospice as she cared for her own aging mother. Once she decided to involve hospice, it made life so much easier for all of us.

When my mom saw my needs increasing and remembered the kindness and help hospice provided, she wanted that level of support for me, too. It was a hard subject for us to broach but once we took the emotion out and talked about it in a practical sense, we moved forward.

The average hospice patient enters the program with a six-month life expectancy. So far, I've been on hospice since September of 2015. I'm re-evaluated every 60 days. As long as they see something that qualifies me for hospice (e.g., weight loss, breathing levels declining, increased anxiety, loss of motor functions) they can justify keeping me in the program.

We've experienced many benefits from hospice. Nikki, my CNA, (Certified Nursing Aide), has become invaluable for Jeff and me. I was nervous about having a stranger care for me in such a personal way. When I communicated this concern to the nursing staff, they said, "It may be your first time, but we've done this hundreds of times." In other words, my tush was not their first tush.

Nikki comes to our house two to three times per week. She gets me ready for my day by giving me a shower, getting me dressed, and doing my hair. I love the hairdos she creates. I am the envy of many of my friends. It turns out she is so good I often tease Jeff, "BUT that's not how Nikki does it!" He just loves that.

My nurse, Rhonda, comes once a week to check my vitals and ask about any needs I might have. This gives me peace of mind to know how accessible my doctor and nurses are to me. In addition to physically being there for me, they fill all my prescriptions, and keep me well stocked with "the good stuff." Most of my equipment and medical needs are now supplied by hospice: Trilogy breathing machine, suction machine, shower chair, feeding tubes, syringes, gauze, and more.

The hospice group we chose has a music therapist on staff. He is available for the patients as well as their families. We thought he would best serve Philip and his needs. Initially he came frequently to build rapport, and now he's on an as-needed basis. It's been an opportunity for Philip to express himself in a nonverbal and nonconventional way. They sit together and talk while playing drums and guitar. For children as well as adults, music can be very healing and a way to release emotions.

Recently, I connected with the music therapist intern and she now comes every other week. For about 30 minutes, she sits in my room, plays guitar, and sings songs of my choosing. For me, her sessions are relaxing and emotionally soothing.

Hospice also has social workers and clergy for my family and me. I see my social worker once a month and more frequently if needed.

NOTE: *I highly recommend you speak with your doctor about whether or not you might qualify. Every area is different. Ask around. You have the right to interview different agencies and select the best fit for your needs. Personally, we chose Seasons Hospice and have been very pleased with their services.*

CHAPTER 13: Unofficial Words of Wisdom

Jenni with her prized hummingbird painting,
looking for guidance.
(8 years, 10 months after diagnosis)

*Now time for a brief intermission
from my side of the story.*

*The following three chapters are
brought to you by my sponsors:
Philip, my son
Jeff, my husband
Joyce, my mom*

CHAPTER 14

The World According to Philip

Joyce (a.k.a. Bubbi; a.k.a. my mom)
Interviewing Philip at age 9

Philip, tell me what you think ALS is?

It's a disease where you cannot move or walk.

Your helper has to help you with everything. My mom has ALS, and I don't think she deserves it.

How do you feel about ALS?

I feel sad for the people who have ALS because they are going through a lot of pain, and I just want to ask others to help them.

What are some of your earliest memories you have of your mom?

When we were in Hawaii going swimming and she did not have ALS. I remember her wearing big fat plastic goggles.

I also remember lots of snuggling with my mom.

What do you think life would be like if your mom did not have ALS?

We could play more often.

We wouldn't argue as much.

We argue because my dad doesn't get enough sleep. I start crying when I'm mad or don't get my way and my dad reacts to that. It would be very different if mom didn't have ALS. My dad would not have to work as hard as he does now. So we wouldn't get in as many arguments.

What are some of the best things about your mom being in a wheelchair?

We don't have to stand in line at the airport.

We go straight onto the plane.

And some of the worst things?

That she can't play with me or anything like that.

But at least she can talk.

Do you ever think about your mom being gone?

Not usually, I don't.

But I do in my dreams. Sometimes a stranger is here and he tries to take my mom. I punch the guy in the face and it always works.

He dies. Then my mom comes out of her wheelchair and I catch her and throw her to my dad. This only happens in my dreams, not in real life.

What do you think life is like for your mom?

She likes everything in her life. Sometimes she gets frustrated and sometimes she doesn't.

She likes hanging out with me, my dad, and my cat and my dog, Piper, and her mom, my Bubbi.

What is your mom able to do?

She can talk and move some fingers. Just one and it's the {laughing}, the middle finger. At least she is nice and she can talk.

What do you think your mom misses?

My mom wants to squish my butt. It's kind of weird. But I would rather let her squish my butt than her have ALS.

Do you feel sorry for your mom?

Yes, I do. A lot.

What would you like to say to your mom?

Mom, it's fine to have ALS because at least you can talk. Most other people who have ALS can't talk. Be happy because it's a miracle.

What other miracles would you like?

To be an NBA player.

To be the best engineer I could be.

Do you think your life is good?

Yes.

What is the best part?

When my friends and family play with me.

To have food, shelter, and water.

What is the worst part?

Sometimes life goes wrong for everybody and I just don't like that.

What do you think your mom would really want you to do for her?

I think she would want me to do my chores and listen to my dad and her. Then I would get an X-Box or things like that. Good things come to those who are nice to their parents.

How could you help?

I could exceed expectations in doing my chores, like doing the dishes without my dad asking, picking up the dog poop in the backyard. Usually my dad has to ask me over and over again.

Why don't you do it without asking?

I'm usually mad. I had a bad day. Probably because I didn't get all my work done in school.

How does it make you feel that your dad has so many responsibilities for your mom?

I think he feels a little tired.

How does it make YOU feel?

Not that good, he has to do all the work.

Sometimes it makes me sad.

What is one thing you would like to change about your mom?

I wish she never had ALS.

If you could change one thing about your dad, what would that be?

Not letting him get so angry.

What makes your dad get angry?

Sometimes when I complain that he is not paying attention to me. He has to pay attention to mom. Even though I am an only child I would like more attention.

Do you get angry?

Angry with my dad.

What does he do that makes you angry?

Makes me do stuff I don't want to do.

Is it safer to get mad at your dad not your mom?

Yes.

Because my mom can't argue with me. My dad is stronger. She already has ALS and she doesn't need any more stuff.

Do you have any fears?

When it is pitch black and I can't see anything.

What would you tell another child whose parent has ALS?

It's all right if you feel sad because I have a mom who has ALS. I just try to do everything that is right for her.

Try to do everything that your mom wants you to do. So your mom feels happy and doesn't get upset with you. She doesn't need that experience. Try to do some special stuff for your parents so their minds can lose ALS.

What do you mean by "lose"?

They won't think about ALS any more. They will forget about ALS and focus on their kid more. My mom and dad care more about me than they care about ALS.

If you do stuff that makes them feel good and not worry about ALS, they can get back into their everyday lives and be themselves.

What do you want to say to your mom's helpers?

Thank you for helping my mom because now she can be proper with anybody.

What do you mean by "proper"?

She can be herself. She couldn't do stuff because she was going through a lot of pain. The helpers are helping her to be normal, like going to the grocery store. My mom asks for help and the helpers do it.

She loves having helpers.

Also she didn't have a strong voice but now she has a microphone to talk.

How has Piper, your family service dog, made a difference for your mom?

She helps my mom with picking up stuff and other things. She is a wonderful dog. I love her.

How has Piper helped you?

I get attention from her. It makes me feel good. I love attention. Piper is the dog I get most attention from. I also get attention from Romeo, my Bubbi's dog.

What do you think about answering these questions?

Pretty fun.

What do you think about having a chapter in your mom's book?

I want one.

Anything else you want to say in the chapter?

No.

Who do you think is going to read it?

You.

Mom.

Who else?

I guess a lot of people. Maybe a million.

How does that make you feel?

Good.

Anything else you want to tell the world?

Hey world, I am so awesome and everyone should agree with me. {hehehe}

Anything else you would like to say about ALS?

I'd say to my mom, "You are the best mom I ever had. You are the only mom I ever had."

I hope I do not get ALS.

There, I'm done! :-)

Can I have a snack now?

CHAPTER 14: The World According to Philip

Philip, age 13 months, first lessons in basketball, gazing at the hoop across the street. Portland, OR (3 months before diagnosis)

Age 2, Seattle, WA (7 months after diagnosis)

Age 20 months, snorkeling, Hawaii (4 months after diagnosis)

Age 3 1/2, playing basketball (2 years, 5 months after diagnosis)

Romeo, 2 months; Philip, age 4

Philip, age 3, Piper, age 2 1/2

Age 3, love of basketball continues

CHAPTER 14: The World According to Philip

Age 7
Indianapolis
Pacers
basketball
game

Age 5 1/2

ALS Ice Bucket Challenge at Philip's School

Age 7 at basketball practice

Age 8,
playing
basketball

Age 8, playing soccer

Age 10,
driving
Grandpa
Sy's boat

CHAPTER 15
A Touch More than Jeff Bargained for

One of my greatest gifts when it comes to living with Jenni's ALS has been my poor memory. It is hard to get upset at life if you struggle to remember the hardships that have occurred. I do not deny that Jenni has lived with ALS for these many years. I do not deny that this disease has made our ability to experience the world challenging. But what I know today is that I do not remember what life was like without this disease, so it is difficult for me to reflect on a time when life was better. My poor memory makes it hard to keep score.

For me, keeping score means remembering what someone has done or something has happened to upset me. If that upset builds up enough points, I lash out. ALS has taken so much away: hugs, back scratches, free massages, getting hit in the arm when I tell a bad joke, being able to relax during intimate moments. Even now, as I write, if I reach far for memories of having a healthy partner and look back on those moments, a bit of frustration and anger comes up. Over the years, as Jenni has gotten weaker, we have had to replace normal intimacy with me taking Jenni to the bathroom in the morning, after lunch, midday, early evening, and possibly twice right before bed . . . not to mention the periodic urgent midnight wake up. My inability to keep score, most of the time, allows the late night wakeup calls to be greeted with humor like, "ALS is the best," or "ALS, a disease that keeps on giving."

Somehow through all of this, Jenni and I have managed to remain good friends. No easy task, I must say. Jenni has this amazing gift of being able to let go of her physical control of the world and direct everyone around her to achieve her needs. I, on the other hand, regularly misplace my keys and wallet.

You can imagine how frustrating it is for her to direct me. For example, she might say, "I am hungry, will you please make lunch."

And I will say, "Sure, after I finish with this e-mail."

Ten minutes go by.

The e-mail is long gone and there Jenni sits, waiting patiently for me to remember lunch. Finally, she sends a gentle reminder my way. Oh, I do not like being reminded, because I did not forget, I got a little distracted. Yet, she still loves me. She still is able to laugh at and with me.

I am her husband and more: I take her to the bathroom; give her multiple showers during the week; feed her breakfast, lunch, and dinner most days; brush her teeth; dress her; undress her; lift her at least 14 times a day; style her hair; put lotion on her face; tweeze stray chin hairs; just to name a few. At one point in our lives, I was brushing Piper our service dog's teeth, Philip's teeth, Jenni's teeth, and my teeth.

I am a better housekeeper, grounds crew, and maintenance man. Thanks to Jenni, I went from the sloppiest kid growing up to a person who enjoys seeing a clean countertop and kitchen table, and she, too, appreciates my effort. I mow the lawn and take out the garbage, recycling, and food waste. I take both our cars in for routine maintenance. I get it: it's a lot of "I do this" and "I do that." But you see, writing it all down feels like keeping score, and I do not keep score too well. I rarely ever think about or remind Jenni about what I do. Somehow I am just able to "do" and I don't expect much in return. Selflessness has not come easily, but I am thankful for this trait or gift. I picked up this skill through participating in high school sports—thank you South Bend Riley Swim Team.

I will do just about anything for Jenni and Philip. Believe me when I say "just about anything"—I draw the line at cutting her nails.

Let's explore selflessness. My life is no longer 100% about me. I rarely have more than one pure hour of time to myself, and even that happens maybe only once every three months. When that moment does come, I seize it.

Most days, I can carve out time for myself by going to the bathroom. The door locked, those precious few moments, I do something just for me. Just getting this time alone was difficult at first. It took serious training for family members to recognize just how valuable this time was to me. Philip would walk in without knocking to ask me to make breakfast "now." Jenni might drive her wheelchair into the doorway checking in on me. Perhaps I overreacted a bit when these intrusions took place, but I felt the need to protect something that was all mine—bowel movements.

Beyond these few minutes of getting myself ready in the morning and those precious bathroom breaks, my time, from awakening to going to sleep, is about Philip, Jenni, and work. Philip usually wakes up early and is ready for breakfast. I'm there to get his day started. Like a typical high-energy child, homework is not one of his favorite activities. I am often confronted with tears when enforcing this dreaded task.

Since I am not getting much sleep at night, my composure doesn't usually reflect that of a compassionate and loving father. I try to be understanding, but when it comes to meltdowns, I don't respond well. Poor Jenni, frozen in bed, has to listen to Philip and me argue for 15 minutes. When bursts of rage come out of me, all she can think is, "When I die, is this how it's going to be? I can't leave this earth with these boys like this."

As soon as Philip is off to his school or camp, I go into the bedroom where Jenni waits to get ready for her day. I give her a chance to laugh at me for my shitty parenting skills. I might say, "Well, at least he said, 'Bye Dad. I love you.'"

Jenni, in these moments, grounds me. Reminds me, that yes our life sucks with ALS, but that does not mean Philip has to bear the burden. I don't like how I am with Philip, and as Jenni says often, "You have so much compassion when it comes to me, I wish you could save up a bit for our son."

For the past five years, Phil and I have gone at each other. But as I write this chapter, he is turning a corner. Our relationship has improved dramatically. Do I deserve credit for this positive development in our relationship? Was it Philip making the shift? What I do know is our relationship feels closer to "normal" than it ever has before.

After recovering from getting Phil out the door, with the help of my mom and Jenni's getting him to school, I turn my focus to Jenni. I work out of our house, so work easily starts to rear its head. Thus I am a bit distracted when I begin Jenni's routine. Typically she has to say, "Jeff, Jeff, I will wear . . ." and of course my mind is not at all focused on the task at hand. I want to work, yet my wife needs me.

Many times I get back in the moment, but sometimes I have to fight with myself. I want to be productive, do my part for my company, get an idea off my chest, yet that has to wait. I must be responsible. I must help Jenni out of bed. On these mornings, I wrestle with my life, even if it is only for a few minutes. And sadly, Jenni will see me "going through the motions." On these mornings, she feels like an anchor; I allowed my mind to drift to an easier place.

I wish I could always be selfless all the time, but I mess up. People want to know how I get by. Well, sometimes I fail miserably. It happens. No matter how I react to my situation, it will not change the fact that Jenni is lying in bed waiting. It will not change the fact that this is our life.

On those days, I eventually get turned around, focused, and ready to begin the next part of the day. We pull together Jenni's clothes, clean her face, apply facial lotion, clean out her nose, brush her teeth, prepare and serve her food, and now we are ready to use the bathroom. After about five minutes of watching *Amy Schumer, Game of Thrones, House,* or whatever series she is consuming to distract her from her thoughts, we are ready to play Barbie.

Our routine has evolved. We started with me just helping pull up her socks, but as she got more unsteady, I started pulling up her pants, and then pulling her shirt over her shoulders. This led to helping her get off the toilet, all the way to closing the deal after the bidet does its job. Through all of the many transitions of me taking over Jenni's typical morning routine, I have managed to keep myself together, for the most part.

People come up to Jenni all the time and tell her how she inspires them. Though I am not nearly as popular (and for good reason), people will come up to me and say how they "admire" the husband I am. They, mostly men, usually say, "I love my wife and I don't know if I am capable of what you are doing."

I think about what's happened during the past decade. I can see how I have been on autopilot and don't consider the fact that I do have a choice to stay in this relationship. I love Jenni. She is my friend, my wife. This is why I am here.

But back to my typical day: Jenni is now dressed, yet not quite ready. We have hair to do. For the first two years of getting

Jenni pulled together, I was stuck playing the role of hair stylist without a clue of what I should be doing. Jenni had visions, but she had me as the artist. Her hair was my least favorite part of our morning. She was not happy with the results and I could not stand doing the same thing day after day.

I broke. I decided for her birthday to get styling lessons, just to find a way to make the morning a bit better. It worked. Before, I never quite understood why a woman would stand in front of the mirror for so long blow-drying her hair. As a swimmer, I keep my hair no longer than a half-inch. With long hair you are talking about drying inches and inches of thick wetness. Through my tutoring sessions with Laura, I gained respect for what it takes to bring hair to life.

I put these new-found skills to work. My morning dread turned to a morning of creations and pride. Straight, curly, blown out, pulled back, I am sure there are others, but I don't know the names. Jenni now had options, and I had something to look forward to that both of us could enjoy. I looked forward to our routine again by turning what had become mundane into something interesting and, for me, new. I am certain that she appreciates my effort, and as selfless as taking the classes may seem, it was selfish.

Once Jenni is ready, I am able to start my day by 10 a.m., which gives me until 4 p.m., when Philip gets home. This leaves enough time for me to focus on work, working out, having lunch, taking Jenni to the bathroom twice, feeding her, and dealing with any other personal items that might come up. I have discovered new ways of being efficient.

Sidebar—You might be wondering what I do for a living that delivers such flexibility. I am an Insurance Archaeologist; I help my clients find their missing insurance policies so that they can make claims they should have made over 30 years ago. I am a part owner in my company, *Restorical Research, LLC.* I work with two amazing partners who are quite understanding of my situation. And I work with many attorneys. One in particular is compassionate and goes out of his way to make sure I know the deliverables he expects from me are not "urgent."

Because of all the "Jenni lifts" that I do in a day, my legs and back hurt. So in 2013, in addition to swimming I began TRX workouts. TRX allows me to complete a strength-building workout in 15 to 25 minutes. In 2015, my hips started hurting, so after consulting with our friend, Lisa, a.k.a., Our Cruise Director and curator of ideas, I took up yoga at The Yoga Studio and began doing lunges. Each day I try to do one of the following activities: swim, TRX, yoga or lunges. I find the more I work out the less pain I am in, making me a better caregiver, husband, father, and worker.

Once the workday ends, I welcome Philip home from school and start dinner. Jenni and I do our best to get a sports-oriented boy to complete his homework. As I've mentioned, this type of expectation is usually greeted with pushback. After getting Phil off to school and a full day of caregiving, projects at work, a workout, and pivoting toward dinner, I have little tolerance for resistance to school work. Again, I am short on compassion. My tired body and mind can only take so much.

What I have going for me is my poor memory. I can only "feel like I have been here before" when it comes to Philip's reaction—I am unable to recall a specific day and time I felt run over because "reading is too hard!" Though I may not be able to keep score, I know that this is an ongoing battle. I know that I am tired. I know that I am about to put my foot down, right or wrong, and it is going to cause upset. I am exhausted.

You may infer there is no light at the end of this tunnel. And perhaps that would have been true but for the many volunteers who come to our rescue: Jenni's Villagers and Helping Hands, all of the courageous friends, family, and acquaintances willing to share portions of their day to help our family. Some make us a meal; others drive Jenni to appointments or on outings; some are skilled, and volunteer to help with a building project or to videotape Jenni for future reflection. They might take her for manis and pedis, shop, take walks, reminisce, or be a juror for a Heartland Film's Truly Moving Picture Award.

With these true helpers throughout our days—and day after day—I have enough time to swim or focus on work or do what I need to do to take care of me. I am magically given the space to clear my head and prepare for the night ahead. Though it may not seem like much, these generous people unknowingly give me the energy I use to get through the rest of *my* day—which means Jenni and Philip will get through theirs, and my family will remain whole.

These microheroes give anywhere from one day a year to twice a week to our family. They come with different hobbies, interests, and represent a range of ages. From amazing quilters to musicians, dedicated community volunteers to corporate employees, they have one thing in common: they love seeing Jenni. When we were dating, I knew she was filled with humor and thoughtfulness. Her willingness to bring people to our table is one of the many reasons I fell for her. It's another reason I continue to choose to love her each day.

When we moved to Indianapolis, Jenni could have easily shied away from people, embarrassed by the toll the disease has taken. Instead, she competes in triathlons and then throws a party for having won the wheelchair division. She brings over a hundred people to celebrate milestones, drawing attention by wearing the most stunning dress. Make no mistake: my ability to wake up and be mentally engaged in our relationship each day has to do with her radiance. This glow is the reason we are able to celebrate our lives with so many people and convert them, eventually, into our "personal bitches" (I mean this in the most endearing way).

What is it about this energy that draws people to Jenni? As an outsider, you may see the hard work that goes into maintaining her quasi-independence. What you don't see is her drive to be engaged in life. For example, when we moved back to Indiana, Jenni, being 18 months into her diagnosis, chose to open up a medical practice. Her passion since living in Australia 2001, has been naturopathic medicine. Patients came to her in their most desperate state. For three years, she worked with them and helped them achieve "impossible" results.

This gave Jenni juice. In the spring of 2014, she decided she wanted to compete in a triathlon. Just like any healthy person would, she set a goal and started working toward it. The *Indy Star* saw a great story in this athletic pursuit. The newspaper article coupled with the Ice Bucket Challenge that was taking off meant, *poof*, Jenni became a local celebrity. This made our lives exciting. She commits to growing through her obstacles, developing herself through projects, and the results are that people want more of her. Just look at her eyes, her dimples, her willingness to laugh at herself. How could you not want more?

Like any human being, Jenni can be a real shit sometimes. Yes, even she can get testy. She might not like how I am putting her clothing on her and will, out of nowhere, head butt my chest hard. I might be touching her hair too much and she is already on edge so she will make a weird "araaarr" sound while pulling her head away from my hands. I might be feeding her too slowly, or not answering one of her questions quickly enough, or my driving is not satisfactory, or sometimes, it's nothing at all.

Yes, sometimes even we can spend too much time together. I am opinionated, so I don't let her attitude go unnoticed. I might say, "Boy, your head sure does weigh a lot," or "So, ALS got ya down?" or "Somebody is a crankasaurus rex." I assure you, if you heard my inflection, you'd know I wasn't condescending, just being a husband. Usually, my comments are enough to break through the ice and the monster disappears.

There are times when Jenni and I will want to slow down, and relax. The moment we are about to rest is when Philip will burst into the room. Just like his mother, our son goes after life. He never sits still, always asking "What can I do?" or "Who can I have dinner with?" or "Play basketball with me," or "Can I go with . . ." Philip is the perfect child for our family. He is constantly pushing Jenni and me to hang with people. Imagine two reserved adults and one gregarious and persistent young man. Whose voice is louder and most likely to win? Not only is Philip not embarrassed by his parents, except when I try to sing his favorite songs, he insists that we be seen with him.

In so many ways the relationships that we have today are a result of Philip. When he walks into a room, you know it. When I walk into a room: "Hey, there's Philip's dad." We throw parties at my folks' house (Barb and Charlie, my mom and stepdad), and realize that we know most of the families because of Philip. Many of Jenni's closest friends are connected through Village Montessori, Philip's first school in Indy. He is the constant source of entertainment . . . never a quiet moment when Phil is at the table. He loves people and he continues to show Jenni and me the importance of togetherness. With Philip, ALS manages to take a back seat. He seems to not care about the disease during most of the day, as his mantra is, "Ain't nothin' gonna slow me down."

What if ALS were not in our lives? Such an easy game to play for all three of us. Philip often says how if his mom did not have ALS, she would pick him up. There is so much that we have lost in her ability to parent, to shape our child in subtle ways. Volunteering at school, mother and son date nights, her lying next to Philip as he drifts off to dream, vacations, eating together without the stress that Jenni might choke. I can whip through dozens of "what ifs" in less than ten seconds. I am acutely aware of what this disease has taken every hour of the day.

I know families must go through their lives thinking nothing of a mother bending down to kiss her boy on the cheek before he goes off to school. I know Jenni would give anything to be that mom. I know Philip craves a mother who is physically capable of such a sendoff. I know the motor neurons, necessary for such a gesture, stopped firing years ago. So I don't often play this game. It causes me to cry.

There are only five times that I can think of that this disease has brought me to tears. At Jenni's request, I delayed my search of ALS on the Internet. Once given permission to surf the web, I quickly arrived at a number of websites covering her eventual deterioration. I tried to visualize Jenni's future path, but I could not get there. When I spoke to my mom, there was a bit of denial and great sadness. My brother Doug, a doctor, could not stop telling me how sorry he was and tried to link me up with his network of professionals. Even when I heard the doctor's final diagnosis, I did not feel the weight of the words spoken.

I remember the first real tears so well. I was driving south to Salem, Oregon, on I-5, speaking with my friend Beth on the phone. It was a few weeks after the diagnosis. Talking with Beth, I began to verbalize what life with ALS would mean for my son. All our future events as a family flashed before my eyes, and I cried.

I do my best not to judge myself for what may seem like a lack of emotion. The first time we heard the words "18 to 24 months" to live, it was palpable. But, for some reason I decided not to buy into the prognosis right then and there. Jenni seemed so healthy. She was a doctor, ready to take on the sickness in others. She was sprinting toward the completion of her GYROTONIC® trainer certification. The sex was great, damn it.

Nothing was going to stop our relationship. And, as it turns out, nothing did. Our intimacy has grown along with our appreciation for one another. To outsiders, my lack of sadness may be perceived as cold. To me, it is a matter of focusing 100% on the present. Maybe it is more like 95%, but I work hard to not take my eye off the Jenni I have now. The Jenni I have now is here, guiding me with observations on how to improve my parenting, directing Philip on how to make good choices, and finding ways to make others laugh.

My "seize the Jenni" strategy is working, but many have suggested I seek counseling. They insist that speaking to a professional will in some way benefit my life. When things get really tough, I vent to my mom, brothers, and dad. Perhaps it is unfair to stick them with all the negative energy I need to offload, but they aren't complaining. I could take my feelings to a career therapist, but instead I have chosen to leave my stress in the pool. Swimming three to four thousand yards two or three times a week helps. Indy Aquatic Masters is my couch with seven convenient locations.

Yes, I have tried talking to a trained ear. However, it seemed that I was expected to do all the talking and I don't talk very much. The feedback there is typically silence. I found myself coming close to making feelings up just to fill the air and use up the hour. Every time I went, I felt uncomfortable. When I relayed my experience to friends, the response was, "You have to find a therapist you like. Keep trying." That may be true, and I may be shortsighted, but I do not want to invest in the effort anymore.

Where does this leave Jenni and Philip? If Jenni's progression leads to her passing away, am I mentally healthy enough to care for Philip during that first year? So many unknowns.

What I do know is this disease got us organized quickly. Upon diagnosis, we sought out an elder care attorney. We wrote our wills and advance directives. We thought through who would care for Philip if our lives were both taken early. We discussed the right guardian to watch over Philip's financial situation. And we discussed the possibility of either of us needing a ventilator should something tragic occur. Though I cried, a second time, it felt good to make these important decisions that otherwise would be left to our parents and siblings to make.

Next big decision: where to bury our remains. A decision we should have made within the first year of moving to Indianapolis, we put off for five. We chose the south side of Indianapolis, only three minutes away from a great cold corned beef sandwich on rye. Yes, Shapiro's is less than a mile away. I am Jewish . . . what can I say?

It's hard for me to believe that one day Jenni may not be with Philip and me. She seems to speak of it with certainty. Am I naïve? On occasion I am forced to consider this possibility. That I may have the responsibility of being the sole parent. That I may have to venture into the world, once again, alone.

It scares me. Yes, there will be many ready to provide support, but those same people will be dealing with their own mourning. Jenni and I have talked about her passing. What my life will look like hours, days, months, and a year out. We have read wonderful books that talk about the way Jews mourn the loss of a loved one. There is a religious formula for grieving. What makes the entire conversation possible is Jenni being willing to acknowledge and contemplate her fragility. I would never bring topics up like, "What would you like your funeral to look like?" if she did not already indicate she was capable of such a conversation.

It is a relief to be with someone comfortable enough to discuss what life after death will look like for our family. It's soothing to think that in some way Jenni will continue to direct my decision-making once she is gone. The type of ALS Jenni has is not moving through her like wildfire. This ALS, still destructive, has given us the time to realize that we can ask questions of each other. Questions that relate to our son's development. Questions Jenni is answering on videotape.

It feels better to know that Jenni will have a say in how to respond when Philip's heart gets broken for the first time or that Jenni is the one to begin teaching him the importance of respecting women. We hope that Philip appreciates, later in life, not only this book, but also these taped sessions. We have heard from other adults who lost parents at an early age that they crave having some understanding of what their parents might have said to them. Jenni, not afraid to admit that ALS could take her life, is working with strength and courage to let Philip know how much she loves him.

If we had kept score during this terrible disease process, all three of us would be on some sort of antidepressant. Sadly, this disease is not a game or a book with a happy ending. My wife is not going to wake up from this dream. Her legs are not going to push her up to attention, her arms are not going to wrap themselves around her boys, and her lungs will not be pushing air into any balloons to celebrate. What Jenni has done with her friends and family is show us all what it's like to live a life in the most selfless way a person can, through teaching. She wrote this book to educate others on how to overcome adversity. She put into writing how others living with ALS can remain independent as long as they can. She provided to everyone who seeks it the opportunity to get to know a woman who squeezed out every ounce of life she had and left it on the court.

CHAPTER 15: A Touch More than Jeff Bargained For

Jeff & Philip, Hawaii
(4 months after diagnosis)

Jeff & Philip, age 2
(8 months after diagnosis)

Jeff & Philip feasting on IN-N-OUT Burger®
(2 years, 4 months after diagnosis)

Jeff & Philip
Strike-a-pose

Jeff, Philip & Jenni
Pre-Indy 500 Race Party
(3 years, 2 months after diagnosis)

CHAPTER 15: A Touch More than Jeff Bargained For

Jenni, Jeff & Philip
A bicycle built for three
(5 years, 3 months
after diagnosis)

Jenni giving Jeff a free ride
(7 years, 3 months after
diagnosis)

Jeff, doing
Jenni's hair
(6 years, 8
months after
diagnosis)

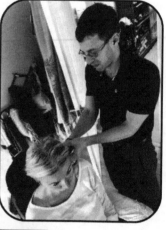

Jenni, Jeff &
family
(6 years, 9
months after
diagnosis)

Jeff, & Jenni
(7 years,
3 months
after diagnosis)

CHAPTER 16
ALS from a Mom's-Eye View

The ticket to life, idle in her pocket.
She misplaced it years ago.
A heart too open and broken
to brave the unknown.
She was sewn tight in a grip
of hurt and deceit.

To be the seamstress
of mending and sending
to the moon of glory,
I unravel your story.
Words of pride
Hands untied

Stretch, Woman!
The sunshine will melt the fist-like expression.
Sobered by the warm light,
Awakened by the musty smell
wafting from her pocket.

Time to live
Sacrificed and forgiven
Loved and never forgotten.

- written by Jenni for me many years ago

Being a companion with Jenni on this part of her journey
and helping her capture her thoughts, experiences, insights, and
distinctive sense of humor for this book has been an honor and a
privilege. Besides the pride I feel for who Jenni is in the face of
adversity, it has brought me an immeasurable amount of joy to
participate in helping her make a difference for so many. I
wouldn't trade one minute of the time I've spent with her in this

process of creating and writing her book for anything in the world, except, of course, a cure for ALS.

When she asked me to write my own chapter, initially, I was equally thrilled and overwhelmed. I had so much I wanted to say, yet had no idea what to say. Where would I begin? What could I add to this already incredible book? I guess, first I'll start with the fact that, as I am sure you can imagine, so much has changed since 2009. Who I was then is not who I am now. Life today is nothing like I, naively, thought it would be.

To put things in context, I have always felt like nothing bad would ever happen to Jenni. Even though she was shy growing up, she has always had an inner resourcefulness. To me she is an "old soul" who knows how to deal with whatever life hands her. In the years leading up to her diagnosis, Jenni was living in Portland, Oregon, and going to medical school to become a naturopathic physician. She was eating right, exercising regularly, taking care of herself holistically—basically doing everything we are told to do to be healthy.

My son Robbie was another story. He did things that made me worry. He became an officer in the Navy and was deployed to Afghanistan during the escalation of the war. When he was stationed in Palau he learned how to scuba dive in shark-infested waters. He attempted to ease my fears by telling me the waters were so well-balanced that sharks were not a problem. He even sent me a picture of himself and a shark in the same frame. I reminded him I was on a "need-to-know-basis" and this was something I did not need to know.

When stationed in Hawaii, he learned how to surf, sharing the water with unfriendly sharks. Oy! While surfing he broke several ribs. He stopped surfing for several weeks, but the love of surfing called him back too soon, thus he re-injured himself, repeatedly! Next, while living in California, he took up snow boarding. One day, high in the Colorado mountains, he took a fall and landed full force on his face, which swelled beyond recognition. Rushed to the hospital, he didn't remember who he was until the next day.

Yes, it was Robbie who could leave me one worried momma, but not my Jen-Jen. I always had the sense that she would be fine.

I also had a selfish reason for expecting her to stay healthy. She had made me a promise. While working as an activities director at a nursing home, she experienced what it was like for people to grow old. She did lots of fun activities with the residents to fill their otherwise lonely hours. She sat with a few as they took their last breaths. If not for her, they might have died alone. Her experiences there led her to tell me, "Mom, don't worry. You will never be in a nursing home. I promise, I'll take care of you. You will live with me."

Thank you, Jen. I love the thought, but fate had a different path for us.

Fast forward to Saturday, March 7, 2009. I remember the call that night like it was yesterday. I had returned from a cruise earlier that evening. I called and left Jenni a message to let her know I was home. When she returned my call, all I heard on the other end was crying. I asked her what was wrong. It felt like an eternity until she finally said between her sobs, "Philip is okay." After more tears as I continued to ask what was wrong, she said, "Jeff is okay."

Philip and Jeff were okay which left my only response, "Then what the hell are you crying about?"

After a lot more sobs, I finally said, "If you can't tell me what is going on, you are going to have to put Jeff on the phone."

She took a deep breath to compose herself and the only words she could get out were, "I'm not."

Now my tears joined hers. I don't know how long we both cried. No words, just more and more tears. In my world, I couldn't imagine what would be causing Jenni so much upset.

She was a healthy 33-year-old. AND she was a naturopath! What could be so wrong? But her tears, her sobs, and her two words, "I'm not," let me know that something life-altering was happening. I just had no idea how altering it was going to be.

Between my sobs I kept asking, "What is wrong? You've got to stop crying and tell me what is going on!"

Finally Jenni pulled herself together and said, "I will tell you, but first you have to promise me you will not look it up on the Internet. I mean it! Promise me!"

I had no idea what I was promising but I knew two things: Jenni would not tell me anything until I agreed to her conditions, and Jenni knew me very well, so if she told me not to look it up, then I knew it was best for me to comply. Whatever "it" was I had no choice but to promise her I'd do as she wished. Jenni called on her inner strength and did her best to calm herself and for the first time she filled me in on the persistent symptoms she was experiencing. She then told me about her visit with Kate and finally the appointment with the neurologist.

First there was the shock, then denial, then guilt—I had been on a cruise while my daughter was going through a living hell. Then I went into a complete panic from not knowing what all of this meant. I just knew that it wasn't good: I had no idea of the magnitude of what I would understand more fully in just a few days.

Jenni then told me she was returning to the doctor on Monday to get her MRI test results. I asked if she wanted me to fly in. She was in Portland, I was in Indianapolis. To my complete surprise, Jenni said yes. Her yes told me volumes; this "it" was really bad. Jenni and I are close, but she is also independent. Normally she would have been adamant that I not jump on a plane to be with her at a difficult time.

When Jenni was pregnant with Philip, I wanted to come to Portland and be a part of the delivery. She vetoed that. I could come to Portland, but I could not be at her house during the delivery. She was planning, with the help of a midwife, to have a natural home-birth. She knew she was committing to something that was likely to be intense. She needed to be strong and independent and call on all of her inner resources. If I was there, she was afraid she might revert to being my little girl, not the strong woman she would have to be. Also, she did not want to worry about me worrying about her.

So when she said she wanted me to be there on Monday for the test results, I knew that what was about to happen was beyond anything I could imagine.

I got off the phone and I went straight to my computer, NOT to look up ALS, but to book a flight to Portland. I left the next day in a completely numb state of mind. Before leaving, I called one of my business partners to tell them I was going to Portland on a one-way ticket for a medical emergency. I didn't know when I would be coming back and I asked them not to call. I requested that they manage whatever needed to be done on their own and promised I would tell them more when I could.

The trip to Portland was about as bad as a trip could be and not just because of what I was afraid awaited me there. When I arrived at the Indianapolis airport on Sunday, I discovered my departing flight was delayed indefinitely. It was coming from Chicago, and Chicago was experiencing a major winter storm. In an instant, my numbness was replaced with panic. I told the airline representative that it was an emergency. I had to get to Portland!

Fortunately, there were two seats left on a flight to Portland via Las Vegas. One other lucky passenger and I happily boarded a completely full flight. Unfortunately, it wasn't until we arrived in Vegas that we discovered our flight to Portland was delayed, stranded by the same storm in Chicago. My fellow re-routed passenger tried to find another option and almost got us on a flight on another airline. I say "almost" because after running as fast as we could to catch the train that connected the terminals, holding our breath as the train moved at what seemed like a snail's pace, then running like crazy to the very last gate at the end of a very long corridor, we didn't make it. We got there moments after the airplane doors were shut and no amount of begging would get the ground crew to re-open the plane's doors.

This shared frustrating experience bonded my new friend, Chaim, and me. Together we would spend many more hours waiting for our Portland-bound flight to arrive. Much to our chagrin, in the city that never sleeps, the restaurants in the airport do. They were all closed. We finally found some snack food in a newspaper strand that was about to close. With our nibbles in hand, we found one of the last areas left to sit. We settled into our spots on the floor, in a far corner of the airport. Resigned to our shared fate, we munched and talked to pass the time. Chaim asked me why I was going to Portland. I had not told a soul what Jenni had told me on the phone the night before. But this young man seemed safe and caring.

I started talking and didn't stop for hours. I probably repeated myself a million times. I told him how my daughter told me not to look it up on the Internet and how I honored her request. I talked about how little I knew about ALS and what it meant that my daughter received this diagnosis. I told him all about Jenni; her life in Portland; the degree she had recently received; my grandson; every detail about her life that was now destined to change. He listened so intently. He was kind. He was a gift. I needed to talk about what was happening but, at that point in time, I did not want anyone I knew to know.

Finally, probably only minutes before we were going to board our long overdue flight, I asked him what he did. He told

178

me he was a physician. Wow, this man knew facts I would soon learn, but he never gave any inkling as to the fate that awaited my family. Not a single facial gesture revealed all the knowledge that hid behind his caring eyes. What an amazing amount of self-control and kindness.

Our flight arrived in Portland Monday morning around 6:00. Exhausted, we said our good-byes and went our separate ways. I look forward to one day finding Dr. Chaim and thanking him for being my guardian angel. Thank him for being a very kind soul who helped me pass some excruciating hours.

The taxi from the airport got me to the Berebitsky household just as they were waking up.

A few hours later Jenni, Jeff, and I were in the doctor's office listening to him tell us that all the tests had come back negative. Naturally, I said, with obvious relief, "That's great!"

If a test is negative, it means whatever you were looking for isn't there, right? He looked at me like I was crazy. Then he explained that negative results meant that his initial diagnosis stood—Jenni had ALS.

My next question was, "Okay, now what do we do?"

Again he looked at me like I was crazy. It seemed like an obvious question so I wondered why he wasn't answering me.

I asked again, "What do people who get an ALS diagnosis do?"

After a painfully long time he looked at me and coldly responded, "They have 18 to 24 months to live. That's what they do."

My emotions went berserk. I was numb—I was crying—I was numb again—I was in denial—I was praying that this was a bad dream and I would wake up any minute—then crying again. How does one cope with this kind of news?

Later that afternoon Jenni and I had a screaming fight. I have no memory of what it was about. In hindsight, I realize it was pent-up emotions that needed a release. We were so angry at what life was handing us.

Finally, in the midst of our yelling I said, "I don't want you to die."

She said, "I don't want to die either."

We then cried and cried in each other's arms.

I have no idea how we survived the next few hours, days, and weeks. But somehow we did.

Two days later we were in Dr. Goslin's office. We were there for additional testing. I thought it was to prove that Jenni did not have ALS; instead, the appointment was to see how far the nerve destruction had progressed. As we sat across from Dr. Goslin she looked at me, then Jenni, then me again. We were about to find out that she was a much more compassionate neurology specialist.

While still looking at me she said, "If it was you, I would have no doubt it is ALS. But she's so young. I just can't believe it. Young females are the rarest category of those diagnosed with ALS."

This would not be the last time a doctor would assume I was the patient when they saw the two of us together. If only it were true . . . I have often wished I could save my daughter from this horror; if only it was me instead of her.

As per Dr. Goslin's recommendations, Jenni spent the following three months having tests: blood work, MRIs, CTs, X-

180

rays, spinal taps, and more. ALS is a diagnosis of exclusion. After an exhausting three months, every test came back negative. We were left with the original diagnosis—Amyotrophic Lateral Sclerosis.

During those months, while my hopes, wishes, and intentions were that the additional tests would rule out ALS, I only told a very select few people about her diagnosis. I made a decision that I did not want the universe to repeatedly hear Jenni's name and ALS in the same breath. My self-imposed isolation took its toll on me. I started to build a very substantial wall around myself. I felt I needed a wall to survive, yet it was also a wall that left me alone to deal with so much uncertainty. In hindsight, I can see that it was not a good idea. At the time, I didn't know what else to do. I had tunnel vision. I had to protect Jenni. I had to find a way to fix this and make it go away.

Not knowing what else to do and feeling like I had no one to turn to, I shut down. I was broken, and I was sure I would never be able to pick up the pieces of my life.

After the diagnosis was official, it didn't take long for me to realize I couldn't keep this secret any longer. I cautiously started sharing Jenni's diagnosis with a few friends, but discovered the walls I securely built around my emotions crumbled far too easily. I couldn't talk about what was happening to Jenni without bursting into tears. Again, I found myself avoiding people. It seemed easier to stay quiet than to face their reactions to my despair. My own grief was all that I could handle.

Initially, the wall was a shield to protect my fragile emotional state. In turn, it served to protect others from my intense outbursts. In retrospect, I wonder if this building process may have caused people to think I was cold, even angry, or at best distant and aloof. If so, that was not the case. I was desperately learning how to cope and doing all I could to survive.

To add insult to injury, when I made an effort to venture out from behind my wall, people often said the most insensitive things. For example, one of Jenni's peers approached me to say she had heard about Jenni, and she wanted me to know how upset she was.

I replied, "I know."

She indignantly came back with, "You have no idea how upset I am! I'm Jenni's age and have a child, too—this could happen to me!"

Standing there with my raw emotions exposed, I was completely dumbfounded. Speechless, all I could do was walk away.

As people heard about Jenni's diagnosis, they would ask, "How is Jenni doing?"

Not wanting to go into details, I settled on a simple response, "Fine."

To my utter amazement they often replied, "Great, glad to hear she's getting better."

Seriously? It took all my willpower not to go off into a tirade about what it means to have ALS. A part of me wanted them to grasp the magnitude of this disease. I wanted them to understand the reality and experience how awful it was to know she wasn't going to get better.

As time moved on, I developed more empathy for others' lack of knowledge. But in the beginning, unfortunately, I had no room for what showed up as sheer ignorance.

Don't get me wrong. I completely understand how difficult it is to acknowledge or even imagine the emotional pain. People want to say the right thing but there was and still is no "right thing" to say. I love that they mean well, but nothing can change the reality we face. Jenni is my daughter, my flesh and blood. No words can lessen my grief, grief that only a parent would know.

Many years past diagnosis, I often marvel at how far I've come. I can talk in public, with few tears, about the details of living with ALS. If you had told me eight years ago that I would be able to handle Jenni's disease the way I do, I would not have believed you. I guess, when the chips are really down, I'm stronger than I ever thought I could be.

I hope this doesn't sound preachy, but this is what my experiences have taught me. Often the best way to help is to just be with the person who is upset. Don't try to make things better. Don't try to find the right thing to say. Don't try to fix anything. Don't run away. Just be there, love them, hold them until the current upset passes, and then let them recover in whatever way they need to. Loving silence can show a huge amount of support.

In the beginning, Jenni relied on Jeff and me to be a shield for her. We were protective and only let in a select few. This space allowed her time to develop the inner strength she was going to require to flourish in spite of her disease.

Jenni has taken this life-altering situation and made the best of it. That perspective didn't come easily. Of course, she was devastated. She had amazing plans for her life, plans that were being snatched away from her. She had many meltdowns. And so did I.

Because of who she is, with a lot of work, and with the help of a few seminars, she reached deep inside, creating a renewed zest for life that continues to sustain her. Everyone she touches experiences her light—she radiates enthusiasm and a commitment to live every day to its fullest. And in the process, she sees the best in everyone and everything.

She totally sets the tone for the rest of us.

People have told me I am amazing, they don't know how I do what I do. They say I am so strong, and Jenni takes after me. I don't know where Jenni gets her strength. I would like to think that I contributed in some way. But I'm clear that how I've been able to deal with this situation is based on the way Jenni deals with it.

She doesn't want people to feel sorry for her; she doesn't want pity; she doesn't want people to think of her as "woe-is-me."

With every step of her progression, Jenni's needs have changed. First she needed to be assisted like any adult with limitations. But then her needs were more like those of a child. Finally, her inabilities advanced so far that she became completely dependent on others, like an infant. Her body is no longer hers to control, yet her mind is that of a fully functioning adult—one who is completely capable of knowing what she wants and making her own decisions.

Initially, these adjustments were very hard for me. I had to learn how to balance her physical and emotional needs with her need to be independent. I didn't realize how easy it would be to slip back into mothering or, should I say, over-mothering. The role came so naturally that I also found myself mothering my grown, fully functioning son. He swiftly put a stop to that. Let's just say his upset woke me up. It was clear that I had to figure out how to balance Jenni's downward progression without compromising Jen or Rob's adulthood.

I love being a mother and I always wanted my children to have their own lives. Parenting is like archery. You pull the arrow all the way back, adjust for the wind, aim for the target, pull tighter, adjust again, and then let it fly. All your efforts are wasted if you don't release and let the arrow soar. Once before, I followed my instincts, successfully let go, and my children soared. Now life was making me relearn how to do this all over again.

Being a Jewish mother makes keeping my daughter well fed a priority. As Jenni's swallowing muscles deteriorated, especially after the nasty scallion incident, Jenni declared she would eat "nothing with an edge." I used my creative instincts and experimented with different food options she could tolerate. What has no edge? Jell-O? But Jell-O has no nutritional value. I did my research and found a grass-fed gelatin that was high in protein and other nutrients. My attempts at homemade jello went from "that's gross," to "that tastes great but looks horrible" (no added food coloring), to "I might just serve that at a dinner party." Unfortunately shortly after I reached this point of success, Jenni had given up on solid food, leaving only beverages to keep her tastebuds happy. I rotate through different teas mixed with a variety of locally sourced honeys as an attempt to fill this need.

My path seems to include many life lessons. A particularly hard one is to not take things personally. Jeff and I are the lucky recipients when Jenni loses her patience and expresses her frustrations. People rarely see this side of Jenni but she can get annoyed and be a real bitch (FYI: comment approved by Jenni).

She may be immobile, but she's mastered the art of saying a few words or flashing a sideways look that is pretty clear. You just know she is thinking, "Can't you get this right? Seriously? Surely by now you know what I want without me having to tell you, AGAIN!"

I have learned that these outbursts aren't Jenni being intentionally mean or that I'm a bad mom for not recognizing her every need. They are her way of saying, "I trust your love for me. I feel safe and can let my guard down with you." This lesson is easier to know in theory but a bit harder to remember in the moment. Most of the time, though, if we lighten it up with a joke or wry sarcasm, the tension can be broken.

Through the humor and the pain, I became acutely aware that in order for me to survive, I could not do this alone. I needed support.

I tried the ALS Support Groups. Unfortunately, I was the only mother of an ALS patient there. Others my age were there because either their PALS (Person with ALS) was their spouse or their parent. When they found out my PALS was my daughter, all they could say was, "Oh no, that's awful. That is the worst!" I wanted and needed support but all I got was so much pity that I had to stop going.

Next, I asked the ALS Association social worker if she knew of any other parents in the same situation. There was one she knew of and got permission for me to call her. Unfortunately, this mother lived in the far Northeast and her son with ALS lived with his wife and their young child in Bloomington, Indiana. He had lost his voice very early in his progression. Unable to talk on the phone and having limited financial resources, mother and son were left isolated from each other. We continued to talk about our shared pain. I hung up counting my blessings. Yes, I hate that Jenni has this disease, but this mother's circumstances made me painfully aware that things could always be worse.

Besides wanting to find more resources, I was also left with the dilemma of how do I let our communities know about Jenni. The mere act of talking about what was going on made the ever-present pain even more unbearable.

Then I remembered that my son, Rob, told me how participating in a Walk to Defeat ALS in California really helped him. With this in mind, I called the Indianapolis ALS Association and asked if there was a local Walk. Sure enough, one was scheduled in about six weeks. Next thing I knew, I was the captain of a team and jumped into action. I gathered the e-mail addresses of everyone I knew and created an extensive list. In August 2009, e-mails were sent sharing Jenni's diagnosis and asking for their support in our first ALS Walk.

NOTE: *You may not need it in the beginning, but creating an e-mail list of everyone who says, "How can I help?" will be a great resource when the time comes that you do need help.*

I didn't realize how much the process of doing what it took to create and organize a team was exactly what I needed. I got to tell everyone in an e-mail what had happened without repeating the agonizing details of our story again and again. After the e-mail was out, at least people knew what was happening when they saw me. Some said nothing, while others would ask how Jenni was. At times, the responses were awkward or painful. But the truth was finally out and, in a small way, life was easier.

We asked for donations to reflect the number 18, which stands for *Chai*. *Chai* (חי – pronounced as a guttural "khi") is a Hebrew word and a symbol that means "life." A common Jewish toast is "*L'chaim!*" (pronounced "luh-khi-ehm") which means, "to life!" Eighteen is a popular number that represents good luck. At weddings, bar/bat mitzvahs, and other events (including charitable giving), Jews often give gifts of money in multiples of 18, symbolically giving the recipient the gift of "life" and luck.

We gave our amazing community a way to support us and help the ALS Association. We raised over $5,000 and got the First Place Team Award. It was the most any Indianapolis Walk Team had ever raised up to then. Each year the amount we raised continued to increase. Several years later, I was in awe when Richie Z's Rockin' Walkers showed up and bumped us off the top. They set a new bar, leaping way ahead and taking first place by raising over $40,000 in their first year. The ALS community is filled with generous people. The teams come in all shapes and sizes, representing all walks of life. ALS does not discriminate.

Even with all the support we receive, despair rears its ugly head, often when I least expect it.

There are times that I am at Jenni and Jeff's house and everything is fine: no new upsets, no significant changes in Jenni's health. I leave happy but once I get in my car, to my complete surprise, the tears start pouring. I drive home sobbing. No reason it starts, no reason it ends. In the moment, everything feels hopeless. Once it passes, I try to put things in perspective. I rationalize that these tears are a way for my body to take care of itself, a much-needed release. Mood swings are part of the grieving process.

Living life as a single person compounds the grief. In the quiet of my house there is no one to talk to, to distract me, to hold me, to help me cope with the waves of intense emotions that are inevitable in this journey. Sometimes it feels like the walls are caving in, and I would give anything to have someone there to help hold them back. Thank goodness for Romeo, my therapy dog. He may not have hands, just four loving paws that snuggle and comfort me with his unconditional love. Dog lovers know what I mean.

Romeo has been great, but I needed more. Finding a counselor I could trust and relate to became especially important. Through diligent searching I found the right fit. I wanted someone to be able to listen and guide me through what to do next, someone able to be with me when the thought of taking another step seemed an impossible task. A counselor cannot remove the pain, but they can help you find tools to persevere and endure.

NOTE: *Finding the right counselor is a process. Not all will meet your needs. For example, the first one I went to advertised as specializing in terminal illnesses. At my first appointment with her, without any fanfare, she asked me what plans had been made for Jenni's final days. I replied, "None, it is not the time yet. She was just recently diagnosed." This counselor proceeded to spend the remaining time lecturing me on why I had to do what she was telling me. She was vehement that I would be sorry if I didn't do all of these steps immediately. Needless to say, I left her office distraught and vowed to never return. Don't let this discourage you, continue to persevere. Over the past eight years I have been fortunate to find three amazing counselors through word-of-mouth. All have helped me in this journey.*

I have Romeo, I have counselors, but I continue to look for ways to take care of myself, an important to-do for caregivers.

For me, the more my mind and hands are busy, the easier it is to cope. As a bonus, my busy hands keep me from filling the void with food.

One of the best distractions began as a lark. I have always been crafty and have a love for jewelry. I thought it would be a great idea to learn how to make jewelry and thus be able to rework some of my existing pieces into new finds. To my surprise, this new hobby became my Zen-place. It fills my soul and is an amazing diversion. The joy it gives me is enhanced by the praise I get. It is humbling as well as gratifying to have so many love my creations. From this distraction my newest endeavor was born: JoyEffects—handmade, one-of-a-kind, custom jewelry, mixing vintage with new.

Jenni was my inspiration to pursue this, and I wanted something symbolic of her on all my pieces. I found a little metal flower charm that reminded me of the JenFlower, our version of a sunflower, which we had created years earlier.

Various people have tried to make the sunflower the symbol of ALS. Nothing official has ever come of it. But in 2014, Ann Tudor, a glass artist friend, picked Jenni and ALS to be the charity she wanted to support. She asked us what symbol we wanted. Unanimously, we picked the sunflower. She created beautiful glass sunflowers that we named JenFlowers. We sold more JenFlowers than any other charitable item she ever made. ALS benefited, and we continue to see so many of Jenni's Villagers lovingly wearing their JenFlowers.

Jenni's Village grew out of the ALS Walk, the Indianapolis Sprint Triathlon, and the wonderful group of helpers that surround us. We truly believe that being a village, caring and supporting each other, can and does make all the difference in the world. A village helps make what one is dealing with so much easier. A village circles the wagons to do what is needed. With our hearts, our minds, and our spirits, we join hands—we are Jenni's Village! We gather around Jenni to provide the support she needs and in turn, she supports us with her sense of humor, enthusiasm, and resilience.

As we are in the final editing of this book, I find myself reflecting on whether there is more I want to say. The days spent writing this book will soon become just a memory.

There is a Yiddish proverb my mom used to say. I can't remember the Yiddish words but loosely translated: *Mothers are blessed with a poor memory. They have the wonderful ability to forget the pain of childbirth. If they didn't, we would all be only children.*

I've spent most of my life being frustrated with having a poor memory. But now I realize my perceived curse has an upside. The forgetfulness I had resented has now become an asset. I often wake up and, in a sense, forget the day before. The sorrow, sadness, and pain I experienced are not as vivid as they were. This fresh start allows me to stay present with Jenni. I am able to focus on her needs of today and not be pulled down by the upsets of yesterday. When I'm with her, I am uplifted.

The many months I have shared with Jenni writing this book has been beyond anything I could have imagined. To collaborate and spend such in-depth quality of time with my amazing daughter has been a real gift! Going through Jenni's life with her and experiencing the joy, the pain, the heartache, I am reminded of the one experience that only she and I share—her birth.

Thinking of childbirth again reminds me of my mom's words. In so many ways, I am thankful for the ability to forget the pain, even if sometimes only momentarily, and live in the joy.

I remember one day when Jenni and I were talking about if we had three wishes what would they be. One of Jenni's wishes was to be free from ALS. But, she added, she would *not* want to lose anything she learned from this part of her journey here on earth.

When I reflect over these years since her diagnosis, I realize that I too have grown in ways I don't want to lose. While I can't imagine or don't want to even to try to imagine what it will be like spending one minute without Jenni here with us, alive and full of life, I find comfort in knowing that I gave birth to an extraordinary woman who is touching so many people's lives.

I've spent most of my life being a glass-half-empty person. I was raised with a depression mentality: worrying about all the "what if's" of tomorrow and missing out on today.

I don't know if I'm always a glass-half-full type now, but I am living in the moment. I'm with Jenni, helping her express the wisdom she has tapped into.

The other day Jenni shared with me a dream she had. The day before we had been to a celebration of life for a friend who was an amazing person and a phenomenal artist. Her life was cut too short. Jenni dreamed that Suzy came to her and sat with her at a picnic table; the same table that Jenni's Grandma Phyllis and Grandpa Sy sat with her in another dream she had right before Sy passed. In yesterday's dream, Suzy said to Jenni, "Everyone has a story to tell, but the lives we have lived, our stories are more obvious."

Many years ago when I did the Landmark Advance Course, I created a mantra, one that I wanted to live by. I wanted to be a mirror so that when others were with me they would see their own greatness. Have I accomplished this? I don't know but what is crystal clear is that Jenni sure has!

The experience one has after being with her is a feeling of being more whole, more okay with who they are. Jenni has the amazing ability to see past the surface crap and connect with people and their essence. She believes all of us have our own beautiful gifts that are often tucked away. This is reflected in the poem at the beginning of this chapter that she wrote for me many years ago.

Jenni said in her letter, the one we gave out at the conclusion of our first ALS Walk in 2009, "*My work is to be present and to remind us all of the urgent call to action to live the life we dream about.*"

I believe my part in this journey is to be a support to Jenni, Jeff, and Philip, as well as provide strength for those who have become our extended family. Learning how to balance others' needs without completely neglecting my own has been a challenge, but one that is important. My hope is that my struggles, successes, and insights along the way may help others as they travel through the ups and downs of their lives.

L'CHAIM!

CHAPTER 16: ALS from a Mom's-Eye View

Robbie, age 3 & Jenni, age 7

Robbie, age 5, Mickey Mouse, ageless, & Jenni, age 9

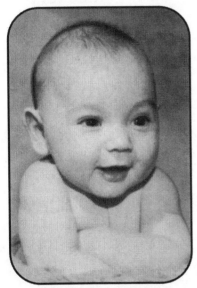

Jenni, age 3 months

Jenni, age 16

Jenni just got her first iPhone. **Thank you touch-screen technology!** (4 weeks after diagnosis)

Joyce & Jenni celebrating Jenni's graduation from NCNM (Jenni, 4 months pregnant)

Joyce & Jenni, Israel 1999

CHAPTER 16: ALS from a Mom's-Eye View

Jenni & Joyce
Lake Tahoe
Weekend met
Les Brown
(3 months
after
diagnosis)

Jeff, Jenni, Joyce, Rob & Gerri
(8 years, 4 months after diagnosis)

Rob, Joyce & Jenni at ALS Walk
(2 years, 6 months after diagnosis)

Rob & Gerri's Wedding
5/9/14

Al, Rob, Joyce & Jenni at
ALS Walk (3 years, 6 months
after diagnosis)

Paris trip 2017

CHAPTER 16: ALS from a Mom's-Eye View

Joyce & Philip,
age 19 months
(3 months after diagnosis)

Joyce, Philip, age 2 1/2,
Rob, Jenni & Jeff
(1 year, 5 months
after diagnosis)

Joyce & Philip, age 9

Philip, age 7,
Joyce & Romeo

Philip, age 9, &
Joyce on Grandpa Sy's boat

CHAPTER 16: ALS from a Mom's-Eye View

Jenni & Joyce at Joyce's
60th Birthday Party
(1 years, 1 month after diagnosis)

Jenni & Joyce at Jenni's
40th Birthday Party
(7 years, 1 month after diagnosis)
Photography: IndyStar/USA Today Network

Jenni, Romeo, age 2 months,
& Piper, age 3 years
(3 years, 3 months after diagnosis)

Joyce & Jenni
Rosh Hashanah retreat
(7 years, 7 months after diagnosis)

Jenni & Joyce
(4 years, 2 months
after diagnosis)

Intermission complete.
Now back to
our regularly scheduled speaker,
a.k.a. Me!

CHAPTER 17
Lordy, Lordy, Look Who's 40!

Friends and family were gathering again, this time for my 40th birthday party. It was a repeat performance for many who had come five years earlier for my 35th birthday party. While that party was to celebrate my outliving my 18–24 months' prognosis, this one was to celebrate full out that I was still here.

Several friends arrived early. Alena, Natasha, and Kate flew in from Portland. Jessica drove down from Chicago. They gathered around me while I lay in bed to conserve my strength. I felt like a princess with my harem nestled around me. It was a treat to reminisce with such dear friends. Alena and I shared stories about our cross-country road trip. We stopped and did yoga sun salutations in every state we went through. The stories, laughter, and lots of shared loved continued for hours.

Although much was the same for both parties (same date in April; same location—The Indianapolis Art Center; same caterer—Matt Mills Catering), my 40th birthday party outdid my 35th. On April 30, 2016, there were over 170 guests; a slide show featuring highlights of my life and the people I love; and an *Indianapolis Star* reporter and photographer on hand to record the festivities.

Adding to the excitement, *USA Today,* print and online, picked up the *Star* article, which led to a video circulated by Humankind.

The glam factor was taken up a notch. My hair was done by Gretchen, a professional hair stylist and friend. My makeup was applied by my cousin Leslie. She had done my makeup for my wedding and years later for Rob and Gerri's. I wore a pink satin Kate Spade dress covered with trendy black polka dots. Sharon customized the dress by adding a stylish "peek-a-tube" opening skillfully disguised as a three-dimensional black rose. My hair was adorned with one of my mom's JoyEffects jewelry creations, custom-made for the occasion.

The birthday party was more like a wedding reception, and the revelers stayed late into the night. Strangers, whose only initial connection was me, left as friends. Most of my family members were there as well as my Village, the people who continue to help Jeff and me with daily life.

"It wasn't just a birthday party. It was more of a thank you," said Jeff. "A thank you to the people whose love for Jenni is in the baskets of folded laundry, the mopped floors, the meal preparations, the trips to the grocery, and countless other mundane chores, all gladly done, and all essential for our lives to continue at a relatively normal level."

The party was fun, the food was great, the service was exceptional, and everyone had a fabulous time. I wanted to thank everyone for all they do for me. And I believe we accomplished that!

As the weekend came to an end, I put the kibosh on goodbyes that tilted toward being overly emotional. No matter what might come, this was a happy occasion, not a final farewell nor a pity party.

I must admit, after the last guest left, exhaustion set in. I used my microphone and speakers but still, people had trouble hearing and understanding me. It was an effort to project my voice as loudly and for as long as I needed. But just as I had at my 35th birthday party, I had anticipated my desire to connect with each of my guests on a deeper level, and I knew that it would be difficult. In lieu of repeating myself 170 times, I wrote another speechless speech that our guests understood loud and clear. See Appendix A for the speechless speeches.

There were tears mixed with smiles as my guests read Jeff's and my speeches. There were gentle hugs and kisses on my forehead. The Helping Hands Blanket radiated its own warmth as it hung from the fireplace mantel. This year there was no dancing but the lively conversations kept the party atmosphere going. All told, this was a night to remember. A night filled with love and laughter. A night of celebration and gratitude.

A night worthy of a chapter in my book!

CHAPTER 17: Lordy, Lordy, Look Who's 40!

Jenni's 35th Birthday Party
KC Goshert Photography

CHAPTER 17: Lordy, Lordy, Look Who's 40!

Jenni's 40th Birthday Party
TOMMY.K Photography

CHAPTER 18

... *until it didn't*

My world spins as I feel the faint wisp of control slip through my
atrophied fingers.
My chest tightens and my lungs betray me.
Damn it.
The brick wall I built around ALS is crumbling.
The emotions spill over.
Desperate thoughts claw their way in,
attacking my heart, my joy.
I feel no peace no strength.
I call bullshit.
The end is scary and messy.
I crave blind faith or ignorance.
I'm helplessly helpless and alone.
I'm afraid the moment I glimpse my reflection
I will crack.
I will crumble.
The pieces too broken to ever be put back together.

- Jenni Berebitsky

As I write my final chapter of this book, I am aware of the picture I have painted in the previous chapters. A picture of me perpetually enduring with no end in sight. In reality, the end now seems closer than I ever allowed myself to imagine. I'm grateful for outliving my prognosis but there are times when I think, "Can we speed this up? How much longer do I have to endure?"

I tire very easily.

To my dismay, my 5'5" body is down to 81 lbs.

Sitting upright in my wheelchair is a major problem. Within moments, breathing is difficult and I need to recline to allow my lungs to fill with air. If I don't redistribute my weight by raising my legs, the pain in my bottom is unbearable.

Speaking is becoming more and more difficult. I feel like I'm screaming at the top of my lungs, yet no one can hear me. For others to understand what I'm saying, I often have to repeat myself. I often opt to stay silent. No matter how frustrating and isolating this is, many times it's just easier.

I can no longer use the joystick of my wheelchair. With the new system, I can drive using the pressure of my left pinky finger, the strongest finger that remains. This allows me some control, but it is cumbersome and time-consuming. After just a few yards of navigating even the simplest of tasks, like going in a straight line, I'm done. The joystick has been relocated to the back of my wheelchair, so I have to relinquish control to my helper, a.k.a. my back seat driver, and trust.

This loss has been a particularly hard blow. I have learned to be dependent on others for so many things, but giving up the control of my wheelchair has been a huge bummer. Outings I used to enjoy: running errands, shopping, going for walks, and doing otherwise normal things, seem like more trouble than they're worth, and require energy that I do not have.

My new wheelchair-driving trainees are often concerned about hurting me. However, it's the shelves of olive oil, wine, and other breakables as well as the unsuspecting door frames that have my attention. I am perpetually concerned about all the potential "whoops" that could happen with one tiny steering mistake. The lucky ones who have had the "privilege" of driving me have a new respect for the skill it takes to drive a six-wheeler.

I thought I was scraping the bottom of the barrel of what was possible when my left pinky finger started to betray me. I reached out to Audi, my wheelchair vendor from Numotion, to see if any adjustments could be made. He came to my rescue. He introduced me to a small local company named Magitech. These innovative engineers are in the process of designing a system for me to be able to drive my wheelchair in a way that I never thought possible. It is a tiny sensor, about the size of an eraser, that is worn in a headband. It will allow me to use my head as the joystick. Very slight movement of my head, calibrated to my own abilities, will give me full access to driving my wheelchair again. I can't wait for the good old days of freedom.

Freedom is a relative term. Living with ALS and relying on your spouse as your primary caregiver can blur the lines between roles. Am I Jeff's wife or his patient?

Jeff and I have always been able to be frank about difficult topics. His matter-of fact-way of being has opened the door for us to have deep, needed, and otherwise heart-wrenching conversations.

"What do you want on your gravestone? Where should Philip go to middle school? If you go unconscious, do you want a vent?"

We've also talked about him remarrying. He's reluctant, but I'm persistent about his future being full and happy.

I'm grateful for this candor and his ability to suck the emotion out of any conversation. But sometimes honesty can be brutal. No matter how painful, we've learned if we stick with it, and call in help when needed, we come out stronger and have a new level of intimacy.

I've lived with ALS for eight years now, and I cannot help but feel bittersweet as I read the recent news and Internet chatter about different ALS "cures." It's like walking a tightrope of hope. People make claims and I don't know what to do. I mentioned these new options to Jeff to hear what he thought and his response took me completely off guard.

Without hesitating, Jeff said, "If you are going to try

anything new, we will need to hire a full-time caregiver. I need my life to be normal. I will take work trips again. Philip and I will go on vacations. And you and the caregiver will become like one person."

I was devastated by his comments. This was more than the two of us could get past by ourselves. We called Mary, our hospice social worker, for help. She listened, acknowledged my upset and Jeff's upset from upsetting me, and then guided us to look at the situation from a different perspective.

Being accustomed to Jeff doing everything I need, I was shocked when he put his needs first. Jeff has taken on the role of being my caregiver so effortlessly, I lost sight of the fact that he's also my husband and I am his wife.

Mary helped me see this by shifting my role from patient to wife. I was able to recognize my responsibility in looking out for Jeff. His needs are important. We are both living with ALS. He has a choice and I don't. At first, that thought made me resentful. But then I realized he does have a choice and he chooses me.

When we stripped away the sadness and hurt, we were able to unpack the meaning behind Jeff's frank words. His role of caregiver was overshadowing his ability to be my husband.

Being my caregiver has altered Jeff's love language. In the past, he would express his love with exquisite gift giving. He relished the ingenuity and time it took to create something special and uniquely individualized to the recipient of his gift.

While I was a student in Portland, Jeff sent me weekly love letters on onion skin paper typed on an old typewriter.

A great example of Jeff's ingenuity was my engagement ring. I had heard a story on NPR about a new discovery. Scientists were able to put peanut butter (a long carbon chain molecule) under immense pressure and create a diamond. I was enthralled by this discovery and exclaimed to Jeff, "Now that's the kind of diamond I'd want!"

Fast forward to the night Jeff proposed. Unable to find a true peanut butter diamond, he hired a glass blower and a metalsmith to fashion a ring.

Jeff said, "I wanted to give you the ring you would never forget and together we would buy the ring you will always wear."

He placed on my finger a silver ring with a giant glass bulb on top. Within the bulb was a charred spec of peanut butter. Charlie, my father-in-law, in describing what a perfect fit we were for each other, said, "Only Jenni would ask for a peanut butter diamond and only Jeff would try to find it for her."

I don't unwrap many birthday gifts anymore. Over the years, his gifts to me have evolved from material objects to generous forms of love, such as literally cleaning up my shit. Of course, there were the creative gifts of learning to do my hair as well as pulling me across the lake for the triathlon. These gifts have not gone unnoticed.

Gifts are one of the many things that have changed in my life. About a year ago, I started having panic attacks. They seemed to come out of nowhere with no particular trigger. Through a lot of soul-searching I realized that they did have a source. I was mourning the mounting loss of control in my life. Becoming aware of this, as well as upping the dosage of my Zoloft and adding Ativan for acute moments, enabled me to lessen their frequency.

As the Serenity Prayer states, "God grant me the serenity to accept the things I cannot change; courage to change the things I can; and wisdom to know the difference." There are things in my life I can control, and some I just have to let go of.

I am going to die. We are all going to die. My expiration

date may be more predictable than others, but we are all heading to the same end destination. What I needed was to come to grips with my fear of what dying will actually look like. How will it feel? Will it feel like drowning? Will I be able to hear conversations around me? Will it go fast or slow? Will it be painful? Who will be there? And on and on.

It is time to prepare: to ask difficult questions of my rabbi, doctor, and social worker; communicate painful but important requests to my family; accept the reality that I have ALS and that I am not playing the role of someone with ALS. It is time to control what I can control.

After many conversations with my hospice doctor and social worker, I feel at ease that I will be comfortable at the end, but will I be unconscious or not? That is a question that nobody can answer. Another unanswerable question, what happens after you die? Oy vey . . . so much uncertainty.

Once again, I have the choice to give up or move forward. Still committed to not being a victim of my circumstances, I have reinvigorated myself by taking control of what I can control. I started making plans.

My mom and I had visited a funeral home years earlier but left without making any decisions. Now I was ready. I felt that one of the biggest gifts I could give my family was to have the arrangements made. So Jeff, my mom, and I went again to the funeral home, this time visiting both cemetery options available to us. The Northside cemetery appeared to be flat and boring. The real deal-breaker came when Jeff found out the land adjacent was recently sold to Walmart. He put his foot down and said he would not spend Eternity next to a Walmart parking lot!

We decided on the Southside Kelly Street Cemetery. Along with the beautiful old trees that offer peaceful shade and grave sites dating back more than 150 years, there was an added plus. After visiting the cemetery, one can easily stop at Shapiro's Deli, just a mile away, and get one of their famous corned beef sandwiches. This was a deal-maker with Jeff's seal of approval. Together we picked three adjacent plots under a welcoming tree. There was no grief, just relief that we had invested in our future and purchased property on the Southside of Indy.

I started having my friend Heather video record me speaking "words of wisdom" to Philip. Speaking into the tape was not as hard I as thought it would be. However, deciding what to talk about was the challenge. The most inspired video was the one in which I told him how he should treat women. Basically I said I would haunt him from the grave if he ever did anything to disrespect a woman.

Another thing I could control was what would happen to my stuff. Who would get what? I started making a list that I entrusted to my mom and Jeff to make sure my worldly possessions would get to their designated new homes. It gives me pleasure to think about my friends treasuring "pieces" of me after I'm gone. Rumor has it I have cute clothes and jewelry.

Indiana is the home of my body but the Pacific Northwest always felt like the home for my soul. It feels comforting to imagine a part of me being there for Eternity. Since I've chosen not to be cremated, the next best transportable part of my DNA would be my hair. I've asked my mom to carry out my vision. Approximately one month after I pass, she is to take my hair to Seattle where she will meet up with Tessa. The two of them will travel to Forest Park in Portland, Oregon, and have a celebration of life as they let my hair go free. It will be an opportunity for my Northwest friends to say good-bye and for ME to be a part of the Forest forever.

These are the plans for after I'm gone, but I'm still here. I need "carrots" to live for, to give me purpose and to give my life meaning. Our philosophy has been to *plan* three months out and to *live* thirty minutes at a time. These have been realistic timelines for us. The three months is not too far but far enough out to keep us moving toward the future. The thirty-minute philosophy keeps us focused on the present and allows us to survive the inevitable unpredictability of ALS. If we make it through the next thirty minutes we are good. Even though at times it feels like why bother, I keep reaching deep inside to find the strength to stay in touch with what is real and what is needed to take on another day.

My wish is that my legacy be a reminder to others to live full out and embrace the moments of their lives honestly and with purpose.

Writing this book has made a difference for me, and I hope it has also done the same for you. This is the end for the book but not the end of my story. I have more life to live and so do you.

Thank you for reading and taking this journey with me.

Namaste...

CHAPTER 18: . . . *until it didn't*

2009

The J Team

Walk to Defeat ALS™
The ALS Association
Indianapolis

2010

2011

2012

CHAPTER 18: . . . *until it didn't*

2013

2014

2015

2016

Walk to
Defeat ALS™
The ALS Association
Indianapolis

2017

Appendix A
Speechless Speeches 2011 and 2016
Jenni's 35th and 40th Birthday Parties

Each of my Speechless Speeches was printed and displayed on a 24" x 36" poster board. Jeff's Speechless Toasts were displayed next to mine in 8" x 10" frames.

Jeff's 35th Birthday Written Toast:

I have always been told I am the emotional one in the family. I mean, I could hardly get out the words of "thank you" at my son's first hair cutting without getting choked up. So to stand before you tonight and expect a coherent toast was next to impossible.

Thank you to everyone that came from far and near to celebrate. We are honored to have you a part of our lives and appreciate your overwhelming support. You mean so much to our family and in many ways this party is a "thank you" to you.

Jenni, you are an amazing woman. Your drive to follow your passion is what has brought the two of us together. Without having found Naturopathic medicine in Australia; without having taken prerequisites to attend Naturopathic medical school in Indianapolis; and without moving so far away from Indianapolis to Portland, Oregon, which hooked me for good, we would likely have not been brought together. Your passion for wanting to help others is why we are here tonight, standing together with a future NBA star for a son (assuming his genetics don't get in his way).

I raise my glass to you for the life you give me, the life you brought to me on 11-18-07, and the life we will live together. I love you so much. Please raise your glass to Jenni—happy birthday my love.

My 35th Birthday Speechless Speech:

My first speechless speech!
- Thanks for indulging me . . .
- Inspired by Anne Marie Schlekeway
- My kick-ass role model to KISS MY ALS
- May she continue to soar high and mighty

You came. Thanks! You may have flown, driven, walked or maybe even cycled over here to the beautiful Art Center. I hope you like the spread. And by the way, you look fabulous!

This is such an incredible honor and special evening, and I really wanted to stand and speak a piece of my heart for you, but . . . I'd be sobbing; you'd be sobbing. There are just so many boxes of tissues you bring to a cocktail party. You know? This way is far less messy and perhaps more intimate because now these words are between you and me.

"We must be willing to get rid of the life we've planned, so as to have the life that is waiting for us." ~Joseph Campbell

Well you can say that again. This is the party I planned, but not the life I planned. Yet, it is my life, and these are the facts. Twenty-five months ago a doctor looked my mom, Jeff and me in the eyes and told us I have 18–24 months to live. WTF. Didn't see that one coming; yet it's here, in my face, and it's my life.

We all know I am not average. I work every day to not let my body, my spirit, my love of life, or my will succumb to a statistic or prognosis.

I am, however, not a hero nor is this life easy. It is in fact the hardest thing I could imagine and I gave birth to Philip in our living room. I believe I know hard.

Witnessing my muscles slowly melt away, longing for my once nimble and graceful ways, weathering emotional storms, fighting the shame of an awkward gait, fumbling every morning to dress myself and get out the door with a smile, pining for the days when I didn't fear a floor absent from props to help me back up, feeling vulnerable, dependent, a burden—well it sucks, and that is just a fraction of my daily physical, mental, emotional, and spiritual obstacles.

Now most of you know, I am not one to complain. I do not complain to not only spare you the muttering, sputtering grumbles that could spew like a geyser, but to spare me. I vacillate between denial and despair and desperately dodge the dogma of disease.

Do not fear, dear ones. I do not hold it all in. Safe spaces and sage advice surround me, and on occasion, I am host to my own pity party. Yet, I have no patience for the whimpers of self-inflicted misery. My quest for gratefulness and serenity is steady and on course.

I know with hard and unthinkable struggles come the golden lessons of life. Stripped from my physical strength, exposed to the core, I see the gifts of the universe.

Days after my diagnosis, I had a vision. I saw dewy strands of light suspended from every heart that connected all people at each moment, a vision that could only be seen through the invigorating mist of insight.

I felt a peace, while scared out of my mind. I was enlightened in the pretense we call life. At times, when I'm lucky enough, I step back into the holographic realm of the connected spirit.

I walk the road of my future, and I stop still in my tracks. Moments are monumental and precious. RIGHT NOW we are here together on this auspicious night to honor each other and celebrate the gift that it is to be alive.

I want to thank you all for being outrageous and unreasonable with your love; for holding my hand and not judging me when I slur, drool, fumble or trip; for embracing your own life, passions, and being courageous in the face of all our unknown futures.

In the wake of your courage and support, I live: as a practicing naturopathic physician, an active mom, a fun and inspirational friend, a loving and adoring wife, a supportive and caring daughter and sister. And with your patience, I am learning how to ask for help.

I have been dealt a hand that quite literally was my worst nightmare. And now living my worst fear has awakened me beyond my dreams. By embracing again and again what is so in my life—whether it be anger, fear, love, or gratitude—AND surrendering to the beauty and wisdom that is life, I am not afraid. I am grateful.

And, I am so happy and thrilled for tonight. Thank YOU for being here.

Now blow your nose and get your booty on the dance floor!

Jeff's 40th Birthday Written Toast:

Thank you for being here tonight to celebrate Jenni's 40th. We are pleased to share the evening with you. When Jenni and I were married, we made plans. We were two excited 30-year-olds. We managed to survive our twenties averaging about $15 an hour without going into debt. So, with Jenni becoming a doctor soon and my company seemingly starting to gain traction, we had visions.

On March 6, 2009, I had no idea, understanding, of what obstacle was thrust into our trajectory. No more planning, no more vacations, no more drifting into the future. We were given no more than two years. I melted. But not in front of Jenni. In fact, since we started this journey Jenni has seen me cry maybe three times. Why? I discovered early on that being sad is me looking into the future. I trained myself quickly to focus on what is happening now. And right now, I have Jenni.

We moved to Indiana knowing we would have a few friends and some family around to help. We picked out our house with the rare future in mind. As soon as Jenni got her bearings, she put up her shingle and started seeing patients desperate for miracles. And miracles they were given. As Jenni's strength diminished, causing her to give up her practice, our family found our own miracle. You. Everyone invited tonight plays some key role in helping us manage each day. From thousands of miles away to a few blocks, we are repeatedly shown love, compassion, and a willingness to serve as Jenni's hands.

When it was time to ask for help, what we received was a generous outpouring of support. "I can fold laundry." "I can cook." "How can I help?" "What can I do?" These offers became the impetus for starting Jenni's Village. And what has come from it? Jenni gets to spend quality time with intelligent, thoughtful and caring individuals each day. And . . . this gives Jenni well-needed breaks from me. Could you imagine having to rely on me for all of your needs?

I have no idea how I could raise a son, care for my wife, fold the laundry, caulk, rearrange the garage, hang paintings, walk Piper, clean out cabinets, reorganize the refrigerator, go grocery shopping, chop vegetables, go to manis and pedis, cut and colors, go to the movies, see plays, organize girls' night out, hang lights, right-right-left-left, be a coach, attend parent teacher conferences and family events, and work. For as much swimming, yoga, and TRX that I do, I know my strength pales in comparison to your collective shoulders. For this we are grateful. For this our family smiles. For this reason, Philip, Jenni and I raise our glasses.

My 40th Birthday Speechless Speech:

First thing first, I want to thank you all for attending the five-year anniversary of my 35th birthday party. Alright, alright it's my 40th. My prognosis arrived seven years ago. I never thought I would see this milestone, so everything now and beyond is gravy. Time to party!

For all of you newbies, thank you for coming—I am so glad you have become a part of our village. For all of you repeat customers, thanks for showing up and sticking with me through the good, the bad, and the ugly. I don't work without you.

By the way, this speech is tough for me to write because I can barely thumb it out on my phone and Jeff is trying to help. He keeps staring at me to spout words of wisdom. So bear with me as I bumble my way through an attempt of getting at graceful gratitude and authenticity.

Speaking of Jeff, can we get an amen? That man takes the cake for husband of the year. And he loves cake! One might think he did not read the fine print of our wedding vows. We went from wife and husband to wife and toothbrusher, hairdresser, housekeeper, caregiver, and much, much more. I scored a lady's maid, comedian, and nurse in the body of a swimsuit model. I like to think there is a special place in heaven for Jeff (maybe 26 virgins or maybe just lots of cake?).

Anyhoo . . . back to . . . me.

There is no way around it, so let's get through the sad stuff first.

The past five years have chipped away at my physical self. Basic human actions like walking, eating, and hugging are gone. Even the simple act of brushing a stray hair off my face is now an impossible task. Extracurricular activities like dancing, hiking, biking, and vacuuming—gone (okay, okay, vacuuming I do not miss). The list of sacrifices is long and I could go on, but I won't. I really don't want to dwell on the loss or in the nostalgia of the past.

Speaking of hugging, you may have a strong urge to hug me, but PLEASE be gentle. I know I am irresistible, but I am also very fragile. Kisses on my forehead (in lieu of that bear hug) are a great way for us to have a sweet connection.

In that same vein, forgive me if I'm not very loquacious. Talking for me is like running a marathon. I want to make it to the end of the party, so I will have to pace myself tonight. PLEASE share your news and ask me (mostly) yes or no questions. ☺

Is this sad? Yes. But I refuse to be a victim of my circumstances. There are times when the weight of my situation and emotions is suffocating. This disease is relentless. Yet by some miracle I awaken every day having pushed the reset button. We continue to move forward and make plans. With the help of the incredible support around me, I have accessed an inner strength I never knew I had. That revelation has been a gift.

To live a normal life is ordinary. I live an extraordinary life. There is beauty and humor everywhere. I'm continually learning how to relinquish control, accepting the illusion it is and surrendering to the unknown—oh so tricky. But the more I do, the more I feel peace.

My toolbox for living is wide and deep. One of the seventy volunteers helps me every day; a compassionate nursing team manages my symptoms and medical needs; naturopathic friends keep my family healthy; an author writes my story; hilarious friends keep me giggling; intuitive women stretch, move, and massage my body away from pain; a synagogue with wise and thoughtful clergy guides me through existential questions; a husband who . . . well see above . . . he does everything; a courageous and loving mom keeps me sane; an incredibly generous extended family who is always at the ready; four caring brothers I cherish; a passionate and energetic son keeps me on my toes; and a few really, really awesome drugs.

So let's enjoy the party and our time together. I'm 40! Eat, drink, and be merry. This is my tribute to you—please know, I honor and value you all. Thank you for being here to celebrate with me!

Appendix B
Jenni's Tips and Tools

Medical Devices
- **Trilogy ventilator** by Philips Respironics—Acts as a BiPAP, sip-and-puff breathing assist and ventilator.
- **Suction machine**—Used for clearing excess saliva. I also use to "blow" my nose.
- **Cough assist**—Healthcare's version of a vacuum cleaner.

Sleeping
- Elbow & heel protectors—The ones I use are made out of lambswool.
- Adjustable, motorized bed—Eliminates the need for a hospital bed. We got a split king, so Jeff does not have to be in the same position as me.
- Extra flat pillows come in handy for arm and shoulder support.
- I love my head pillow. It's very soft while holding its form; made from natural latex.
- CamelBak® water hydration bladder—Hung from headboard, allowing me to use the tube to sip water when thirsty at night. This was helpful when I could not longer sit up and drink from a glass.

Hands
- Lightweight locking pliers for turning keys in door
- Wrist brace for stability
- Sewing scissors that fold up real small – use to open packages
- Signature stamp for signing checks and documents
- Tennis ball to rest hand on to keep palm open and fingers unclenched
- Defrosted gel ice packs to protect hands and forearms once your own protruding bones become weapons. My friend Kara's

daughter, Elaine, made me a "pillow case" out of cloth diapers to act as a cover for the pack.
• Kinesiology Athletic Tape (a.k.a. K-Tape) to support my droopy fingers

Feet

• **Foot-Up®**—A lightweight ankle-foot orthosis that offers dynamic support for drop foot or similar complaints.
    https://www.ossur.com/injury-solutions/products/foot-and-ankle/ankle-foot-orthosis/foot-up
• Custom-made strap attached to front of boot
    http://www.theshoefitsindy.com/
• Custom-made sandals.
    http://www.theshoefitsindy.com/
• Compression socks for travel

Wheelchair

• I chose the brand Permobil through the vendor NuMotion. Make sure you get fitted correctly for your wheelchair!!! And get one that can be changed and adapted to your ever-changing needs.
• If you can afford it, a wonderful feature is the seat lift elevator. This gives you the ability to raise your entire chair to adult standing height.
• Select a comfortable seat cushion—You're on your ass a lot! I selected a hybrid model, gel in the back and foam in front and sides.
• Seat covers and cloth diaper under cover—for looks and hygiene (easy to clean)
• Armrest covers to protect your arm from the heat of black vinyl armrests.
• Strap that hangs phone around joystick or armrest
• Cellphone holder
• Trilogy breathing machine attached to the back
• CamelBak water hydration bladder, hung from headrest, allowing me to use the tube to sip water when thirsty.
• To add a little designer flair, I added a decorative stethoscope sleeve to conceal the tubes for my air and water.

- I used a cloth backpack on the back of the wheelchair for carrying needed items.
- Added an easy-to-push switch for changing joystick mode, which allowed me to control the various functions of the wheelchair through the joystick.
- Cup holder
- Be prepared to be creative. One time when we couldn't find a curb cut to get up on sidewalk, we made a ramp out of the snow that was on the ground and added our 12" threshold ramp that we always keep in our van.
- Inflatable camping pillow to add more head and neck support.
- We carry a door stopper with us at all times. Super handy!

Meals

- I am a firm believer that food is medicine. Although the prepackaged feeding tube formulas are convenient, they lack any live ingredients, which is vital to maintain our health and well-being. People often tell me I am the healthiest person they know, except, of course, for having ALS.
- Over the years, I've streamlined the preparation of my meals. Hopefully this information will inspire you to incorporate real food into your feeding routine.
- Using a powerful blender, like the VitaMix, you can make anything into a liquid meal. The basics for each meal include: a healthy protein, about the size of your palm; fresh vegetables, about one cup; and eight ounces of liquid, water or homemade broth. The protein can be chicken, fish, beef or even pork chops. Vegetables can be anything you like, such as: broccoli, cauliflower, salad greens, etc. Be aware, the starchier the vegetable, the thicker the liquid will be, which will make it harder to use with your tube. With chicken I add a teaspoon of sunflower seed butter for healthy fat. You can use any nut butter but I find this to be the easiest to digest. If you use a fattier protein, i.e., salmon or beef, the fat you need is already in the protein.
- I prefer chicken as my protein. The system I devised for ease-of-preparation is: cook approximately 8 pounds. of

boneless, skinless breast and thighs with enough liquid to cover in slow cooker for about 8 hours. I use a box of organic chicken broth as my liquid for the added nutrients and salt. Once cooked and still warm, we shred the chicken with a hand mixer. Next we divide it into 1/3 cup portions, more or less depending on how much you can tolerate per meal. We use individual dry wax paper sheets (purchased at Costco) for each portion. We fold them up and store multiple portions in a freezer bag (approximately 20 per bag). I usually end up with about 50 portions.

• When it is mealtime, we take one portion of chicken from the freezer, put directly into blender and add 4 ounces of hot water from our Instant Hot and 4 ounces of room-temperature water. We then add the veggies, nut butter, supplements, and blend.

• It's important to blend twice and shake vigorously in between to avoid having any small pieces stick to the side, pieces that could clog your tube.

• Depending on the food you choose, some liquify enough to pour and others need to be plunged. If using a syringe to plunge your food, be careful to pace yourself. Pushing food in too quickly might cause indigestion.

• We also add the different supplements I take to the meals we blend.

• Once a day, I have a whey protein shake. I also add sunflower seed butter to this meal.

• I have found eating smaller meals more frequently works best for me.

• Feel free to be creative but remember to use as many fresh, organic ingredients as possible.

• And when on the go, we use Liquid Hope by Functional Formualaries, http://www.functionalformularies.com (which needs to be plunged) or Orgain Organic Nutrition Shakes (which can be poured).

Kitchen

- Create your own environment—Inspired by Montessori education model.
- Dysum – A non-slip tacky material for opening jars, etc.
- Cutting board with knife attached for food prep (see photo)
- We put plates in pull-out drawers in under-counter cabinets for easy reach.
- Electric can opener
- We remodeled our kitchen for easy wheelchair access
- Jar opener attached under cabinet
- Placement of security alarm box—low for easy access
- We added an Instant Hot Water Heater faucet at the kitchen sink. Originally for cooking and making hot tea, but also turned out to be great for sanitizing the feeding tubes.

Bathroom

- Walk-in shower with zero threshold to allow for a roll-in shower chair
- Sink with no cabinets underneath so wheelchair can be pushed all the way up to countertop
- Bidet Toilet Seat offers modesty when you can no longer clean yourself. Can be installed on an existing toilet. Features include a pulsating water stream, wireless remote control, warm air dryer, and heated toilet seat.
- Blow dryer mounted on wall
- I don't have this but it looks awesome: The Only In-Shower Body Dryer, TornadoBodyDryer.com
- Toilet elevator—A spacer that is installed under the base of your toilet, adding 3.5 inches of additional height while still maintaining the appearance of your toilet. This is instead of the more typical riser that sits on top of the toilet seat, which would eliminate the ability to install a bidet.
- Alimed Comfortable Bed Pan—billed as the most comfortable bedpan and it is.
- Widen door frames
- Handle bar next to toilet
- Mechanical toothbrush

- Brushing teeth, support your elbow (either countertop or a tray) to be able to brush independently for longer
- Even though you might think you are okay, always sit or make sure there is a wall behind you to lean on. Take it from one who has experienced it—falls in the bathroom hurt.

House

- Bought a ranch house—one level
- Changed door knobs to levers
- Got rid of entertainment system and put TV on wall (created more space)
- Got rid of throw rugs—Easily caught in wheelchair
- Ramps inside and outside
- Hand railing up to the front and back doors
- Widen door frames when possible. The doorframe to our bedroom could not be widened, so we installed a sliding barn-door instead, giving us a few valuable extra inches.
- Label drawers and cabinets so helpers know where to find things.

Car

- Steering wheel knob for when you are still able to drive yourself.
- Always enter a vehicle seat butt first. You are less likely to lose your balance.
- We've been through three different handicap-accessible vans. Our first two vans had an ATS conversion—reasonably priced. They both had rear-entry manual ramps for the wheelchair. Eventually we were ready to upgrade and decided on an automated side-entry ramp by VMI. This allowed for me to sit shot-gun. In the previous vans, I was positioned behind the front seats and between the two back seats. Rear entry is easier in parking lots but the side entry is better for parallel parking. With each new van we had no problem selling the previous one.
- You are able to use the cost of the handicap conversion of a van as a tax deduction.

- EZ Lock for wheelchair—http://www.ezlock.net/—an electronic docking system that locks the wheelchair into place automatically, electronically monitoring the chair during the van's operation. A simple press of the button releases the chair.
- Seatbelt covers to avoid irritations
- Inflatable camping pillow behind head to soften the bumps
- To prevent being "tossed" around while driving, I recommend an upper body seatbelt that attaches to your wheelchair. Talk to your wheelchair vendor for options.

Transfers

- Gait belt—I use two, one around waist, other under knees
- Transfer Sling, which I call my "flying carpet"
- Slide board
- If able, have a PT or OT come to your house to teach your friends and family proper transfer techniques.
- Pivot/transfer disc—Operates like a "Lazy Susan," rotating the person so they are able to transfer with minimal physical effort. Top and bottom surfaces are non slip for safety. http://www.drivemedical.com/index.php/transfer-disc-683.html

Communication

- To call for help: baby monitor and/or cordless doorbell.
- USB for iPhone attached to battery of wheelchair so can "wake" Siri up by saying "Hey Siri"
- Speaker and mic to help project your voice—I use a wireless, Bluetooth voice amplifier. The Bluetooth serves several functions: 1) it allows me to not have to deal with a cord across my body, 2) people can easily hold the speaker up to their ear and 3) at a big table, I can place my speaker in the middle of the table and "throw my voice" so I'm a part of the conversation.
- Try the Eye Gaze technology. It might be right for you. It did not work for me.

Clothing

- Replace snaps or buttons on pants and shirts with hooks or Velcro. Had buttons sewn to front of pants to hide buttonholes.
- Loops sewn on sides of pants waistbands. I could hook my thumb into the loops and pull up when the rest of my hand could no longer grip the waistband.
- Costume jewelry on key ring attached to coat zipper for easy grip
- Name clothing and jewelry to make it easer for caretaker to know what you want.
- Elastic band pants or cute work out clothes are in style and easier to manage.
- Avoid Stump-the-Chump clothing. This is what we named clothing that was hard for Jeff to figure out how to put on.
- No underwear—one fewer item to pull up and down AND eliminates wedgies.
- No socks—Uggs are great boots to keep your feet warm without the hassle of socks.
- Dress alteration for feeding tube—Adorable fabric to cover openings made in dresses—Peek-a-tube (see photo)
- Poncho coat from the Colts, my local NFL football team—Covers me and my wheelchair in the rain.
- Sandals (never settling)—Custom-designed sandals for ease of putting on and hiding the swelling and color of feet.
- I use tiny nickel-size magnets to attach my shirt to my bra to avoid shirts from slipping off my shoulders.

Travel

- Wedge pillow folds into a rectangle and has a carrying case—I use in hotel beds to elevate my upper body.
- Extra seat cushion for airplane seat. I'm still searching for the perfect one.
- Always bring feeding tube supplies in your carry-on when traveling by plane. Even though TSA says you cannot bring liquids through security, you are allowed to bring your unopened feeding tube food. Just disclose it when going through security.

- Consider wearing an adult diaper for longer flights. Added peace of mind.
- If you make your own feeding tube food: the Vitamix Personal Blender is portable for travel and great for home use, too. Blend twice, shake in between cycles, for optimal results.
- I mentioned this earlier, but again note: Southwest Airlines is far and away our carrier of choice.
- If you are traveling with your power wheelchair, call the airlines in advance to clarify their policies. We have found each airline has its own set of procedures.
- You will be able to stay in your own chair until the end of the gang-way where you will transfer to an airplane aisle chair. Your wheelchair will then be loaded with the baggage. Once at your destination, you will wait on the airplane until your wheelchair is brought back up to meet you again at the end of the gang-way.
- Make sure you know what type of battery your power wheelchair uses and how much the entire chair weighs. Also make sure you know how to turn off the electrical and how to put your chair in neutral.
- Allen wrenches that come with wheelchair in case you need to disassemble any parts.
- We recommend removing the headrest, seat cushion, and any other easily removable, a.k.a. breakable parts. Bring an extra carry-on suitcase to place these items in.
- It is your choice if you want your own wheelchair during a layover. We prefer this option unless it is a really quick turn-around between flights.
- I bring a beanbag neck pillow and inflatable camping pillow for extra comfort onboard.
- Bring a change of clothes.
- Bring baby wipes.
- We have a portable Toto brand bidet we always bring with us on all trips.
- Think through how you want to be transferred from your wheelchair to the aisle wheelchair and then to the airplane seat. Usually, they will ask you what you prefer.

- If you are prone to anxiety, I highly recommend you take your medications preemptively. I'm a seasoned flyer, but traveling with ALS can be very stressful.
- For added comfort, sit in the bulkhead seats. After takeoff, bring one of your suitcases down to prop your legs up.

Mental Health
- Landmark Education—LandmarkWorldwide.com
- Les Brown or other motivational speakers—LesBrown.com
- Counselor or therapist of your choice
- ALS Associations—ALSA.org. From there you can find your local chapter
- Meditational recordings, CD's, podcast, etc.
- Friends—Let them know your needs. Lots of times they may want to help, but just don't know what to do.
- Crying—Let your emotions out. They only get worse if left bottled up inside.
- Jeff—He's mine, you can't have him. ;-)
- Mom—We all have one, but I'm lucky to have the one I have.
- Zoloft—Life is better with the right chemistry.
- Piper—I was lucky enough to get a service dog. Check your local area to see your options.
- Gyrotonics and massage—Move your body and when you can't, have someone else move it for you.

Friends
- We had ramps built at friends' and families' homes so I could easily visit them.
- Lotsa Helping Hands is a great website to use for volunteers to sign up to help—LotsaHelpingHands.com
- Learn how to give up control—ha, good luck—so that you *can ask* for help when you need it and *accept help* from people who are usually grateful to give it.
- Learn how to explain something to somebody without being able to show them how to do it—can only use your words, no hands. A skill that is much harder than one would think.

- Speak in Yoda-speak. Cut out the niceties.
- Say what is most visual first. Example: To explain where my trashcan is, I would say, "Dishwasher, left of."
- People like doing what they are good at. It's a win-win when you pay attention to your helpers' different skill sets and make requests accordingly. People may be happy to help with tasks such as:
- Organizing your home, your family, your volunteers
- Making labels (see earlier suggestions)
- Doing laundry
- Handy-person projects
- Shopping and running errands
- Cooking
- Cleaning
- Yard work
- Being a good friend—Thanks everyone!

Appendix C

Resources and Protocols

By no means am I the only ALS patient, caregiver or medical professional with a story to tell and advice to give. Below is a list of websites:

• ALSA.org—The ALS Association helps patients and families cope with the day-to-day challenges of living with ALS by providing information, resources, and referrals to many sources, including a wide variety of community services. The ALS Association's nation-wide network of chapters and other partners provides localized patient and family support in communities across the country.

• ALSuntangled.com—reviews alternative and off label treatments (AOTs), with the goal of helping people with ALS make more informed decisions about them.

• ALS.net—ALS Therapy Development Institute—the world's foremost drug discovery center focused solely on ALS (Amyotrophic Lateral Sclerosis).

• PatientsLikeMe.com—track and compare symptoms, progression, and protocol results with ALS patients around the world.

• Every90minutes.org—Within in this site there is a technical guide with links to various things to help make life with ALS more productive.

• ALSNewsToday.com—a news and information website about the disease.

• YourALSGuide.com—designed to provide clear information, connect you to resources, save you money, expand your support network, and generally make life with ALS a little easier.

- PerformanceHealth.com—a great one-stop shop for devices and advice.

- ALSFromBothsSides.org—Written by a nurse who has been living with ALS for 30 years. She goes into great detail about some of the medical complications one may face as a result of ALS.

- JasonClementalsFund.com/forpals—Jason's Guide to Living with ALS, from a man's perspective.

- TeamGleason.org—Steve Gleason and his friends and family started Team Gleason to generate public awareness about ALS, raise funding to empower those with ALS to live a rewarding life, and ultimately find a cure. Under their Technology Information section on this website, there is information on how to request assistance in obtaining an AAC (Augmentative and Alternative Communication) device.

Next, protocols. Below is a list of the "treatments" I believe have worked for me. I left out the multitude I tried and saw no measurable results. I am very tuned into my body and notice subtle differences.

Please note, this is anecdotal information. There is no guarantee any of the following will work for you. No scientific tests have been done, except for LunaRich X (Lunasin Regimen), which is currently in a trial: https://clinicaltrials.gov/ct2/show/NCT02709330

~ Low Dose Naltrexone (LDN) (starting dose 1.5 mg, February 2010. Current dose 4.5 mg, increased in 0.5 mg increments).

~ Chronic cerebrospinal venous insufficiency (CCSVI) is a term coined by Dr. Paolo Zamboni of the University of Ferrara in Italy. CCSVI describes a theory in which the veins in the head and neck are narrowed or blocked, and therefore unable to efficiently remove blood from the central nervous system. CCSVI procedure done, fall 2010.

~ Trip to Mass General in Boston to explore various ALS drug trials, Sept 11, 2012. Unfortunately, it was an exercise in futility. The good news and the bad news: I was progressing too slowly to qualify for any of the studies.

~ Mercury dental fillings removed by a dentist certified in proper amalgam removal, spring 2012

~ Specialized intravenous, heavy metal chelation treatments that followed dental amalgam removal, spring 2012

~ G-tube (feeding tube) insertion surgery, spring 2013, and replaced with G-Button, summer 2014

~ Finiti supplement with TA-65 by Jeunesse Global, summer 2014

~ LunaRich X by Reliv, summer 2016

Appendix D
Walk a Mile in My Shoes
or At Least Five Minutes.

The following article was written by Bo Stern. She wrote about her husband and their life with ALS. It captures the experience of living with ALS.

https://qz.com/251372/what-its-like-to-live-with-als/#

The Actual Challenge:
What it's like to live with ALS

People ask me often what it's like to live with ALS. It's a brave question because the answers are not very pleasant. But it's also such a worthy question because understanding how this disease impacts those who suffer from it creates empathy, which is so valuable; it carries us into another person's world and allows us to understand what they're feeling and how they're hurting. As I watch my strong husband struggle with things that used to be easy and automatic, I sometimes wish that everyone could see life from his perspective.

If you would like to experience just a tiny corner of an ALS life, I have a list of empathetic experiences for you. These are things you can do to walk for just a mile in ALS shoes. If you try one, take a little time at the end to consider that people actually living with the disease have a million miles more to go.

1. *Pick up a 10-pound weight. Now imagine it's your fork and move it from your plate to your mouth repeatedly without shaking.*

2. *Sit in a chair for just 15 minutes moving nothing but your eyes. Nothing. No speaking, no scratching your nose, no shifting your weight, no changing the channel on the television, no computer work. Only your eyes. As you sit, imagine: this is your life. Your only life.*

3. *Borrow a wheelchair or power scooter and try to maneuver quickly through the aisles at Walmart, without speaking. Note the way people react to you.*

4. *Strap 25 pounds to your forearm. Now, adjust your rearview mirror.*

5. *Using none of your own muscles, have your spouse or child or friend get you dressed and brush your teeth. Write down some of the feelings you have being cared for in this way.*

6. *Before you eat your next meal, take a good, long look at the food. Inhale deeply and appreciate the aroma. Now, imagine never being able to taste that – or any other food – for the rest of your life.*

7. *Put two large marshmallows in your mouth and have a conversation with your friends. How many times must you repeat yourself? How does this make you feel?*

8. *Go to bed and stay in one position for as long as you possibly can, moving nothing.*

9. *Strap weights to your ankles and climb a flight of stairs, taking two at a time. That's the kind of strength it takes for someone with ALS to tackle the stairs on a good day.*

10. *Install a text-to-speech app on your phone or iPad and use it exclusively to communicate for one day.*

Good Lord, that was depressing even for me! ALS sucks. If you are not overwhelmed enough with her list, here are a few more from my own experience of living with ALS:

- Put on a pair of oven mitts, now try to make dinner.

- Sit in a chair or lie in bed. Have everyone else leave the room or house. No matter what happens, you cannot do anything. See how long you can last. What do you feel? Fear? Panic? Abandoned?

- Have someone put on noise-cancelling headphones. Now try to talk to them. Can they understand anything you are saying?

- Hold your bladder for as long as you can, then wait for someone to come help.

- Next time you are outside and a bug or insect lands on you, do nothing. How long can you last?

- Get in bed and bunch the sheets, enough to create a crease under you. Now lay perfectly still on that crease and see how long it takes before it starts to feel like a knife cutting into you.

Appendix E:

Almost Famous

The following are links to articles and videos about my journey.

~ HELEN RAINE'S article: "ALS WOMEN"
Published September 2014 issue of Pink Magazine
https://helenraine.com/womens-articles/als-on-ice/

~ "Indy woman with ALS: 'By some miracle, I still have my speech'"
Dana Hunsinger Benbow, dana.benbow@indystar.com
Published 3:33 p.m. ET Aug. 13, 2014 | Updated 8:17 p.m. ET Aug. 4, 2015
http://www.indystar.com/story/life/2014/08/13/indy-woman-let-als-keep-triathlon/14014565/

Aug. 14, 2014 Indy Star article

~ "Woman battling ALS to compete in triathlon"
By Dana Hunsinger Benbow—*Associated Press—Thursday, August 14, 2014*
http://www.washingtontimes.com/news/2014/aug/14/woman-battling-als-to-compete-in-triathlon/

~ "Indy woman with ALS turns 40; she wasn't supposed to"
Dana Hunsinger Benbow, dana.benbow@indystar.com
Published 6:58 p.m. ET May 4, 2016 | Updated 7:05 p.m. ET
May 4, 2016
http://www.indystar.com/story/sports/2016/05/04/indy-woman-als-turns-40-she-wasnt-supposed/83561302/

~ "Defying her ALS diagnosis, woman competes in triathlon"
Video:
https://www.indystar.com/videos/life/2016/05/04/14166093/

~ Article about documentary on Jenni being done by
Paul Nethercott, an international documentary filmmaker
"Indy woman in late stage of ALS: 'I feel like a ragdoll'"
Dana Benbow, Special to IndyStar Published 2:37 p.m. ET Dec.
4, 2017 | Updated 3:46 p.m. ET Dec. 4, 2017
https://www.indystar.com/story/sports/2017/12/04/indy-woman-late-stage-als-i-feel-like-ragdoll/918853001/

~ Beloit College Magazine—Winter 2017
Best Friends Forever by Susan Kasten
http://magazine.beloit.edu/?story_id=247336&issue_id=247271

~ USA Today and Humankind video
https://www.usatoday.com/story/news/humankind/2016/05/07/woman-als-turns-40-but-she-wasnt-supposed/83969342/

Appendix F:

Thoughts from Jenni's Villagers

As Jenni's mom, I'm prejudiced when it comes to my daughter. She inspires me every single day. Except for having ALS, Jenni lives a life many people would love to have. She seems like anyone else, yet she manages to make the simplest activities special. Most of all, she has a unique gift of being able to connect with others in the most profound ways. This includes her best-of-the-best trait: she makes others feel special, she helps them see the best in themselves and love themselves. This is how I've always felt about Jenni and it warms my entire being to know that others see and feel the same way. It's not just a mother's bias! I think this is who Jenni was before ALS, but dealing with what life has dealt her has only strengthened her strengths and minimized her weaknesses.

ALS is not an easy journey. It's a "sucky hand to be dealt!" When it enters someone's life, it affects everyone around them. Somehow Jenni has found a way to take the worst of what life can do to a body and not only make the best of what she has, but also along the way continue to make a profound difference for so many other people. This energy and love are what I'd love to capture through others' words.

We are often in situations where we don't know how to act, what to say, how to express ourselves. My intention and hope is that these words will help others find ways to deal with what life has given them or someone in their life and help them better understand that what they say and do as well as their actions affects others—often for better or worse, and not only for a moment or a day, but for months and years to come.

After Jenni's party and the media publicity she received, we've had a lot of people tell us how much she inspires them. We were touched by these comments, but they also made us wonder. What does inspire mean? How were others inspired? What difference has Jenni made in their lives?

These questions turned into an idea, then into an inquiry that has become part of Jenni's book. With Jenni's permission, I sent out an e-mail to her family, friends and helpers. I wanted to know what they had to say.

We asked them:

What makes Jenni "Jenni"?

What about Jenni inspires you?

What about Jenni is so unique? Be as specific as possible.

How has Jenni impacted your life?

What about Jenni makes you want to be with her, do more for her, have her in your life?

How has Jenni affected other areas of your life?

How do you think you are different because of your relationship with Jenni?

What difference do you think you make for others because of how Jenni has inspired you?

Here are the comments we received. Some answered all of the questions, others used our questions as a guideline for their answers. No matter how anyone answered, we completely appreciate the love and admiration they have so graciously shared with us. We profoundly thank you!

Please note: in the interest of space, some responses have been condensed. We tried to keep the essence.

Melisa S., childhood friend

Jenni has impacted my life in so many ways. She has taught me about friendship, unconditional love, and openness to exploring the world and the beauty life has to offer.

When I was diagnosed with breast cancer my world as I knew it imploded. Yet after wrapping my head around things and looking to others and God for strength, I reflected on all that Jenni goes through daily. Seeing her fight and flourish despite every changing obstacle brings me strength and quiets my inner worry. I already knew I was inspired by Jenni but now I know I can have her strength to meet whatever life throws at me head on. I choose to make the most of my life and realize life is precious and fleeting.

Jenni and I both chose professions where we would be of service to others. When I was battling cancer I realized it wasn't just about me. My family, friends, students, and their parents were impacted. I tried my best to follow Jenni's example and remain positive and fierce. I chose not to let cancer break me. People have shared that I have been an inspiration to them. I thank Jenni for being my inspiration. Strength, grace, and humility are more than a mindset, it is a way to live life. Through watching Jenni I have learned how deeply we can impact others and I want to be that positive role model, too.

Barb and Charlie, mother-in-law and father-in-law

After our daughter Kylea first met Jenni, she asked Jeff, "If you and Jenni break up, can I still have her for a friend?" That was our introduction to one of Jenni's defining features: the way she makes everyone want to be near her.

Only a truly exceptional person could collect the exceptional friends and relationships Jenni has enjoyed.

She's everybody's best free doctor.

Her friends from her medical training (and now their families as well) are devoted to seeing her whenever and wherever they can.

The friends volunteering companionship on the "Jenni's Village" list are regularly bumping us from a fair share of her company. (To the point that Charlie has had to threaten legal action for any encroachment on his Thursday PT trips with Jenni.)

Lisa B. and others take turns leading girl outings. Popup parties, trips to Pacer suites, and joint ventures to yet another showing of "Hamilton" are routine.

The parents of Philip's friends are mainstays in this Jenni Circle. And, of course, the Story of Jenni can't be appreciated without noticing the radiance in the Story of Jenni, Jeff, and Philip. Their love and devotion to each other are inspirations—and often endless entertainment—for the rest of us.

And at the center of all of this is the young lady committed to seeing the best in everyone important to her, overlooking our foibles, and celebrating all of life's blessings. She blesses all of us every day, and all we see are people appreciating and jealously guarding their chance to be close to her.

❧❦❧❦❧❦❧❦❧❦❧❦❧❦❧❦❧❦❧❦❧❦❧❦❧❦

Katie D., friend and one of our "Helping Hands"

When I think of Jenni, I think of her twinkling eyes, inviting smile, incredible warmth, and witty sense of humor. I think of her grace, love, and endearment as a wife, daughter, and friend. She is honest, intelligent, and beautiful. Jenni understands, supports, cares, and delights in hearing about her friends' lives.

After my time with her, I feel uplifted, enlightened, strengthened, and grateful for her friendship. She is a gift in my life that I treasure.

Tammy D., friend and one of our "Helping Hands"

Jenni helps me keep perspective in life. She has a laser focus on what's important and is very good at letting the rest go without another thought. She inspires me to do the same.

Her mind is a steel trap and I admire her for that. She knows exactly what she wants and has a plan in her head of how to get that accomplished, whether it's a list of tasks for the day or a long-term, ongoing project.

Barb and Mitch M., longtime family friends

I am 62 years old. I find that I don't have the same energy level, agility or the good health I once enjoyed. Doors close, as they say, never to be reopened. My natural tendency is to be depressed about these changes and, then, I think about Jenni . . . She inspires me to never give up and to find the joy in life.

Gayle B., friend and one of our "Helping Hands"

Jenni speaks a thousand positive words through her silent, uplifting, gentle, and pure smile. What a privilege it is to share precious time with you, Jenni. I have loved every minute!

Donna D., friend and massage therapist

I have known Jenni since she was 16 years old, and have always felt she was an "Old Soul." What makes Jenni Jenni to me is her vibrant response to life on life's terms. She inspires me by living her life full out, regarding her condition holistically, and by not letting her circumstances define her.

I have the pleasure of giving Jenni weekly massage and Reiki treatments, and in doing so, I have received more than I have given. Our sometimes profound and sometimes silly conversations leave me living my life more fully, and cherishing each and every day. Jenni is authentic, bright, kind, fun, and fully self expressed. She enrolls me in her quest to be her best, and inspires me to be my best, too!

Tami K., friend and one of our "Helping Hands"

There is an old Jewish story that reminds me very much of Jenni. In the story, a group of students come to a rabbi quite distressed by the darkness that exists in the world. They are afraid and despairing, and ask the rabbi how they might protect themselves from the darkness. The rabbi gives them brooms and suggests they begin by sweeping the darkness from the cellar. When this does not work, the rabbi gives the students sticks and suggests they beat the darkness away from the cellar. When they are unsuccessful again, the rabbi asks them to shout at the darkness, and once again they fail. Finally, the rabbi says, let us challenge the darkness with light. It is better to light a candle to illuminate the darkness than it is to curse and fear it. And as the first student descended into the cellar with the light of one candle, the darkness disappeared.

Jenni is like the shining light that glows brightly from a candle.

Just like every one of us is faced with darkness in our own lives, Jenni reminds us that it is possible to use light to drive back the darkness. Jenni is vibrant, hopeful, present, and courageous. Jenni continues to teach me to seek light in my own life. For this, I am extremely grateful to Jenni.

∻∻∻∻∻∻∻∻∻∻∻

Tessa H., college friend

I've known Jenni my entire adult life, and she's had a mighty influence on who I am as an adult. I learned how to be bravely honest from Jenni, and all the other amazing things I have learned from her are, you know, amazing, but, learning to be honest (especially with myself) has been the biggest and best. She demonstrated it was okay to be who we were, warts and all, and that allowed me to live more authentically day to day, especially during those times when I have been really uncomfortable with myself, my choices . . . Jenni doesn't judge, and that makes everyone around her just relax and be themselves, their wart-covered selves.

∻∻∻∻∻∻∻∻∻∻∻

Mark S., friend and one of our "Helping Hands"

Jenni burns more brightly than the sun. Her 1000-watt smile forgives me, as I stumble through the steps of trying to drive her to the store. I'm blessed by her grace, for I know, after many lessons, that she will talk me through the most complex set of instructions. Her patience—her poise—remind me to calm down and focus, this day, and every day.

And, like the sun, she exerts a force on so many: we are drawn into her orbit by the force of her personality, intelligence, and love. I recognize others who are inspired and awed. And as Jenni and her family celebrate with us, I (slowly) realize that she, and they, model the way to deal with the unknowable: with love and grit, grace and resolve, gratitude and brilliant smiles.

≈≈≈≈≈≈≈≈≈≈≈≈≈≈≈≈≈≈≈≈≈≈

Kara B., friend and one of our "Helping Hands"

Jenni blends beauty and function into her surroundings—her house, her van, her clothes, her hair. Why does this affect me? I grapple with giving myself the gift of beauty and function. If I want something that will make my life more joyful or easier I debate whether or not I should—spend the money on it, spend the time on it, ask for it, and so on. I recall Jenni's ability to take ownership of what will give her joy, ask for what she wants and get it. This is not about materialism or consumerism. It's about knowing her own mind and heart and pursuing her vision so that she can enjoy life now.

Jenni makes a lot of room for me and my thoughts, emotions, stories, and experiences. I am sometimes embarrassed by how much I talk about myself. But Jenni brings it right out of me. I long to talk to her and tell her about my interior world. Why? Because she gets it—immediately. No translating needed. And she is deeply honest with her own experiences. For me, this is about as good as life gets—a genuine exchange of my lived experience with another.

So for that reason, Jenni is a soul friend.

≈≈≈≈≈≈≈≈≈≈≈≈≈≈≈≈≈≈≈≈≈≈

Lisa B., friend and one of our "Helping Hands"

Jenni came into my life on a beautiful spring day in 2010. She was crying outside the door at the Montessori preschool our sons attended. I expressed concern and she responded, "these are tears of joy." She had just been told that she would be receiving Piper, a service dog from the ICAN program. It was then I learned of her ALS diagnosis. She was still walking and driving at the time, although I remember her coming to my house and needing to use both hands to lift her glass of water.

These are things I know about Jenni:

She is one of the funniest people I have ever met. She is wicked smart. She listens with her whole being and without judgment. You can confess to her your gravest errors, and she will make you feel that your mistakes do not define you while simultaneously inspiring you to be a better human being. When you are struggling with a relationship problem, she is interested, sympathetic, and insightful.

She forgives you for not knowing how to act around her or stupidly saying things like "growing old looks miserable" as a few 70-year-old women walk by your table in unattractive compression hose. If you ask her if you are washing her dishes/folding her laundry/chopping her vegetables the right way (which she would give anything to be doing for herself), she will tell you "whatever way you do it is the right way" and mean it. She can competently talk both trashy television and current events.

She treasures her mother, her in-laws, and her friends. She is proud of her son. She adores her husband and he is her perfect foil. (Jeff, you deserve your own book.)

She will openly share almost any of her many adventures/difficult life choices and when she does it is without apology or regret and with the intent to connect over a human experience. If you are sick she can recommend a fabulous natural remedy. She will always tell you the truth if you ask her if you look fat in those pants. She almost never chooses the same nail polish color twice. She will never begrudge your enjoyment of the many things ALS has stolen from her or trump your legitimate daily frustrations with her disease.

Jenni once told me, "I think everyone has a gift to give the world and that living with ALS is my gift." We agreed that it was a shitty gift, but a potentially important one. She has shown me and countless others how to live with courage, gratitude, humor, and love while her body degenerates and fails. She does not consider herself to be heroic but she does want her life to mean something.

It does, my friend. It does.

I love you and am so grateful to know you.

❧❧❧❧❧❧❧❧❧❧❧❧❧❧❧❧❧

Uncle Al

My niece is an unbelievable woman. She has been dealt a bum hand; yet, she has made lemon soufflé from lemons. Jenni has taken her situation and turned herself into one of the most brave, appreciative, and positive people I know. She lives every day with beauty and purpose. She is more active with her friends and family than I have seen from most people. She has been an inspiration to me, and she is an inspiration to all who know her and have been touched by her. Jenni has always had a smile on her face ever since I knew her as a child. Her smile is infectious. Jenni is a star who provides me with deep and respectful pride. Her life, and everything she stands for, will shine forever.

❧❧❧❧❧❧❧❧❧❧❧❧❧❧❧❧❧

Jerry J., family friend and one of our "Helping Hands"

Jenni has been such an inspiration to me. Since my daughters and Jenni grew up together, I have always felt she was a very special lady. When she was diagnosed I frankly didn't have a clue how to respond. As I watched this horrendous disease consume more and more of her body, I was continually amazed at her ability to adapt and conquer even small portions of her disability. I will probably never forget the first time I had to feed her. I wasn't very good at it, and put way too much in her mouth for her to handle. Of course because I was used to filling my mouth. She eased my discomfort by pointing out how her mother did the same thing and of course it spilled all over her.

Rori G., friend

What I admire most about Jenni is her drive to live her life in the face of this horrible disease. Rather than give up or focus on limits or inevitabilities she has participated and lived her life in spite of her disease. As the physical limitations have increased she regroups, learns to deal with new challenges, and presses on. The letter she wrote prior to the first ALS walk has always stuck with me. She wrote about having had a young baby at the same time as receiving devastating news. She said how she grieved the life she wouldn't have for 6 months but then she got up and continued to live. And she has, fully. Parties, soccer games, pitch-in dinners, break the fast dinners, jewelry parties, movie reviews, and all the little things. Not all of us could or would do this.

For her 40th birthday toast she spoke of how the disease could at times be suffocating. Yet Jenni has managed to maintain her friendships and make new ones, raise her fabulous son, enjoy a loving marriage, and quite simply, live. She is the embodiment of will, mind over matter, and appreciation of life.

I am a better person for knowing her. So how has Jenni inspired me? By being Jenni, plain and simple. Her attitude and approach to life makes me appreciate my life and those around me. It sounds cliché but I am really honored that I am a small part of Jenni's life.

Mark S., friend and one of our "Helping Hands"

Every so often, we are blessed to meet "halo people." These individuals, and Jenni is one of them, have a special quality that make you feel as if God is sitting on their shoulder looking out for them.

Halo people have a practical optimism that is inspiring to everyone whose lives they enter. I believe that when these people are dealt a bad hand in life, their uniqueness becomes even more apparent to those around them.

I will always remember the time I took Jenni shopping at the grocery store. It was like being with a celebrity. Everyone we encountered—whether they knew Jenni or were seeing her for the first time—smiled at her. It was astonishing to behold. People just felt good in her presence.

Like countless others, Jenni has inspired and reminded me that we all have a choice about how we handle difficult life situations. I like to think that if I follow Jenni's example, maybe God will be a little closer.

<hr />

Muriel M., friend and one of our "Helping Hands"

There really aren't words to describe Jenni's uniqueness, inspiration, and the impact she's had on my life. Although our time together has been short and I've only known her for the past couple of years, there are qualities about her which I reflect upon daily. Some are profound and some are mundane and seemingly ordinary, but very special to me.

Of course, the profound impact of Jenni on me is the true realization that one's life is so fragile and never to be taken for granted. Whenever I am facing one of life's many obstacles, large or small, I think of Jenni with wonder and this truly gives me perspective and makes me grateful for what's really important in life. Seeing Jenni and Jeff working together raising Philip and living such a normal life under extraordinary circumstances is inspirational.

I love that Jenni is so fashionable and makes sure that her hair, clothes, makeup, etc., are always just right. I will never forget that great pink dress and stunning hairdo on her 40th birthday party. She has a unique sense of style.

Of course her organizational skills are legendary. When I'm at her house helping, she, in a very few words can direct me to the exact spot on the exact shelf in the exact cupboard where everything belongs. It reminds me of playing the game "Concentration." I'm thinking of hiring her to organize my house and then come over to help me keep it that way!!!

Seeing Jenni's whole family coming together to help her and Jeff in so many ways has demonstrated what true family values are. That reiterates my strong feeling that family and friends are really what matter in life.

Mary Anne L., friend and one of our "Helping Hands"

How do I begin to describe the impact Jenni has had on my life?! Joyce, her mom, and I had become good friends, and she told me about Jenni and her diagnosis. Eventually there was a website that I could sign up on to volunteer to "help" Jenni. But, I must admit, I have always received more help than I have given. I first met her in her office, as she walked across the room and shook my hand. That was obviously, many years ago, but her impact has never left me. Yes, I "help" her by doing laundry, dishes, chauffeuring her, prepping food, following her directions in organizing different things in her home, yet she has "helped" me by her kindness, inner strength, wisdom, listening to me, beautiful smile, sincere warm personality, and, most importantly, love. Her strength gives me strength, her love sends me away loving others even more, her feeling of "presence" helps me to be more "present," her calmness leaves me more calm, and her positive attitude inspires me to be an even greater person. After all, living day to day as she does makes me appreciate my life even more!

❦❧❦❧❦❧❦❧❦❧❦❧❦❧❦❧❦❧❦❧❦❧❦❧

Rita P., friend and one of our "Helping Hands"

I have only gotten to know Jenni in this past year, but wish I had gotten to know her sooner! Her strength, sense of humor, upbeat attitude, and the interest she shows in my life are incredible. With all of her challenges, she takes time to really know others. It really is true what I was told—I get so much more from Jenni than I could ever give. She is truly amazing—and such a love!

❦❧❦❧❦❧❦❧❦❧❦❧❦❧❦❧❦❧❦❧❦❧❦❧

Ed, father-in-law

From the moment I met Jenni I knew that she was a very special person with qualities one does not find often in people. Her wonderful smile, great sense of humor, and beautiful glowing face made me so happy that my son Jeff had found such a special person to share his life with.

Every time I am with her I realize how her extraordinarily positive attitude, spirit, and inner beauty have been a reminder to all of her loved ones and friends on how to live their lives and are confirmation of why she has so many people that love her. I find it so easy to be with her and so much enjoy her personality and friendship. I love her very, very much.

❦❧❦❧❦❧❦❧❦❧❦❧❦❧❦❧❦❧❦❧❦❧❦❧

Debbie M., childhood family friend

I have had the pleasure of knowing Jenni since she was a very little girl. Even then, she was warm and caring. Now, she has become "more so" . . . more caring, more loving, and able to touch more people's lives.

Jenni is a free-spirit, filled with the love of people, nature, and all the little things that happen to come her way. When Jenni smiles, her face lights up from within and she adds a glow to her surroundings and all those around her.

Jenni has taught me about getting the most out of every day, no matter the trials you are facing, and looking forward to the next. A true inspiration and beautiful person, all the way through.

Aunt Kristi

OK this has been very hard, but to put it simply, Jenni inspires me by getting up each morning and putting on a smile.

Jenni inspires me by dealing with this horrible disease each day with more grace and calm than I can generally muster in a month.

Jenni inspires me by her willingness to go everywhere and do everything possible to have a full and wonderful life. I think particularly of her officiating at her brother's wedding, attending Hamilton, and flying across the country to attend her cousin's wedding.

Thinking about Jenni brings me to tears and makes me incredibly grateful that she's part of my family.

Lynn V., cousin and one of our "Helping Hands"

As a Montessorian, I consider and apply the Montessori philosophy in many different ways in my life. But Jenni has taken the application of Montessori philosophy to a whole new level. Jenni learned about the importance of "The Prepared Environment," which essentially means that one prepares a child's environment so that the child can be successful in all ways. So for example, The Montessori Prepared Environment was the first philosophy of education to use child-sized chairs and tables and materials to be used with small hands. Jenni applied this concept to her life in brilliant ways.

Whenever something became difficult for her to do, Jenni devised another way of doing it that made her successful. One of the first examples might have been to install a knob on her steering wheel so that she could continue driving. With each way that Jenni's body began to fail her, Jenni's brilliant mind devised a way to become successful at that task. Along with Jenni's tremendous sense of humor and positive outlook, this application of the Montessori Prepared Environment continues to amaze me and thus to admire Jenni immensely.

❧❧❧❧❧❧❧❧❧❧❧❧❧❧❧❧❧❧❧❧❧❧❧❧

Tammy B., sister-in-law

I just spent a weekend in the Upper Peninsula of Michigan and while I was there I stayed in a tent on the beach. During the first night there I was battling fears of a potential bear encounter—never saw one of those—and then when it was time to go to bed a torrential rain and wind storm began and continued all through the night . . . the tent blew and blew and blew and I was so scared. I thought for sure the tent was not going to survive the night nor me. The next morning after the winds died down all I could think of was how proud I was of my little tent and how it stayed strong through that storm. You have marveled me with your strength and courage and for some reason, my little tent is what came to mind when thinking of you. I love you.

Aunt Susan

Jenni is an inspiration to me when I think the going is tough—and it really isn't. Jenni is an inspiration when I'm tempted to give up on something fairly simple and then remember her sheer courage and persistence.

But, all that said, I love to check out what she's wearing, her latest hairstyle, and her cool earrings and necklaces. I want to know what TV shows and movies she'd recommend, talk politics, and ask for advice on health issues. I want to hear about the great places she's visiting, catch up on family news and stories, and laugh with her. In other words, she's an inspiration, yeah, but the best part is she's Jenni.

Leslie D., cousin

Jenni's attitude toward life and the people around her is something I can only strive to emulate. She is the most open, present, effervescent person that I know. When I feel like I'm straying too far from my ideal path in life, I often turn to thinking about Jenni. She lives a life of authenticity, honesty, and generosity of spirit. Just reminding myself of how she lives her life can usually help me course correct my own :)

Afi, stepmom

I remember Robbie, her brother, telling me that they had asked Jenni to officiate their marriage. I questioned if he was sure about choosing Jenni, since guests could feel sad and focus on her. He politely responded that he would consider it.

Well, I was so happy that I was so completely wrong. When I saw Jenni [officiating at her brother's wedding], it truly was magical. She was like a ray of sunshine coming in and brightening the whole atmosphere. What a wonderful occasion and Jenni was one of the highlights of the night. She had the biggest, contagious smile on her face then and every day. Her attitude is amazing. She is truly inspiring and I am so happy that she has been in my life.

Lori P., Philip's 1st–3rd grade teacher

I have been inspired by Jenni many times over the past three years. Even though I know that it must be exhausting, Jenni never misses a school event to support Philip or school fundraising. From our yearly silent auction and parent-teacher conferences to Philip being promoted to the next belt in karate and basketball games or any other sporting event that he participates in, Jenni attends it all. She has volunteered weekly to read books with students and has even spoken to the students about ALS so that Philip's friends would have a better understanding of ALS and its effects.

I know she reads with Philip and helps with homework even when I am sure she is exhausted. Her wonderful spirit is alive and well in her Philip. She is always smiling and happy spreading the joy that I know lives inside of her. The loving, caring, happy intelligence that she has imparted to her young son, throughout what I am sure have been difficult times, inspires me on a daily basis.

Heather M., high school friend and one of our "Helping Hands"

Jenni and my friendship goes back to high school where I knew by the end of senior year we would have a lifelong friendship. She was fun to be around and we laughed a lot but we also had a connection that went deeper (or I just like to remember it that way!). We talked about relationships, dating, parents, career plans. We kept in touch, sometimes just by postcards, mail from around the world and quick visits when she came home to Indy. I loved her sense of adventure and how she always wanted to learn more. Today these are still a big chunk of why I love Jenni!

My family has benefited from our time spent with Jenni and her family. My kids have learned to not let anything stop them. Together we have witnessed determination laced with humor first hand. When something feels like it's too much to handle we dig a little deeper, maybe make a joke, and push through because we have watched Jenni do the same. I have watched the relationship between Jenni and Jeff and learned how I want to treat people in my life. I know this has changed the dynamics in many of my relationships with family and friends. When I need something from a friend, I ask straight out. When I think someone needs help, I try to offer very specific help: Do you need a meal dropped off? Do you need someone to come do dishes? Do you need a ride?

Jenni is open with her friends and willing to make connections. Instead of shutting down she opens up. This has been amazing to witness and I have made a choice to do the same in my life. I focus on approaching life with humor, adventure, learning, determination, and love.

~~~~~~~~~~~~~~~~~~~~~~~~~~~~~~~~~~~~~

Sara B., friend and one of our "Helping Hands"

Jenni has such an engaging/magnetic personality. People are drawn to her. She is a great listener and says it how she sees it and doesn't hold back. She has wonderfully expressive eyes. She is so very smart and is a great resource for naturopathic remedies.

I have never heard her complain about anything. Although it

may have been challenging at first, she graciously allows those in her Village to help her in all ways. Giving up control and accepting help can be a very hard thing to do, and Jenni is terrific in this way.

The way she can look gorgeous and sweet and pure and then opens her mouth and says the kind of things that would make a truck driver blush. I love that about her, because she can really make me laugh. I always feel lighter and happier after I have been with Jenni.

Knowing Jenni has made everyone in my family better people. My kids have so much respect for her and being around Jenni has opened their eyes to the different challenges that people face. I believe that my children are more empathetic because Jenni is part of our lives. Eli, my oldest son, actually started thinking of inventions that could help someone with ALS.

I think that we as a family are more willing to give to others, both in time and money, when they are dealing with medical/health issues. Knowing Jenni makes you want to be proactive, to make change for the better.

I only met Jenni about 6 years ago, and didn't know her before she had ALS, but I can only assume that the Jenni I know is the only Jenni there is. She is one of the best people I know!

Erin M., childhood friend and one of our "Helping Hands"

I don't even know where to start. I've known Jenni since we were three years old; she was my very first best friend. When we were little, we used to wear our Wonder Woman Underoos and jump off our couch. Little did I know then that Jenni would grow up to be my super hero, my "Wonder Woman." Jenni's strength, poise, and beauty from the inside and out, are remarkable. She continues

*to soar above each crappy hurdle ALS has thrown at her and she
does it with poise and grace.*

*You've heard of making lemonade out of lemons, well, Jenni
makes trendy fashion statements out of ALS hurdles: losing her
ability to easily grasp zippers became a fashion statement with the
use of earrings added to zippers to create cute and manageable
zipper pulls; needing a feeding tube turned into a sense of flare and
fashion with the cute pocket designs she had added to all of her
dresses to make her feeding tube easily accessible.*

*Jenni has not let ALS keep her down, heck her weekly schedule is
busier than most adults I know. And even with everything going
on in her life, Jenni still has time to be a sounding board, giver of
advice, and cheerleader. Jenni shows us how to live life to its fullest
and reminds us what is truly important in life. I am so fortunate
to be a part of Jenni's life and member of the J Team. Jenni is my
Wonder Woman and it melts my heart that she is "Aunt Jenni" to
my three children.*

<del>ଏକ୍ଚ-ଏକ୍ଚ-ଏକ୍ଚ-ଏକ୍ଚ-ଏକ୍ଚ-ଏକ୍ଚ-ଏକ୍ଚ-ଏକ୍ଚ-ଏକ୍ଚ-ଏକ୍ଚ-ଏକ୍ଚ-ଏକ୍ଚ</del>

Rebecca W., friend and one of our "Helping Hands"

*What I know about Jenni: I didn't actually meet Jenni until after
she moved back to Indianapolis, after being diagnosed with ALS. I
first got to know Jenni through her mom, Joyce. We met Joyce in
2007 when we were preparing to move back to Indianapolis after
living in Chicago for many years.*

*And Joyce told me all about Jenni. She said she thought we would
get along well and if Jenni ever moved back she was sure we could
be great friends—which I loved hearing because I was in need of
some new local friends. So when I actually did get to meet Jenni, it
was a pleasant surprise to experience her exactly as her mom had
described her—fun, smart, and like-minded. She also provides a
wonderful sounding board, both for my professional clinical*

practice and my personal life—with levity, clarity, and wisdom.

Uncle Paul, Aunt Deb, Alex, Scot, Shannon, Wyatt, Violet, and Skah

"A Bird Doesn't Sing Because It Has an Answer, It Sings Because It Has a Song."

Jenni is a song! Her courage, grace and amazing heart are an inspiration to us all and we love her with all of ours.

Rabbi Brett, friend and one of our "Helping Hands"

Jenni reminds me that true bravery is not about overcoming fear, it is about feeling the fear and doing it anyway. Jenni reminds me that there is humor to be found in every moment, that we can laugh through the tears, and that laughter heals. Jenni reminds me that strength and beauty are better expressed as perseverance, grace, and grit. Jenni reminds me that life is a journey, that not one of us can afford to waste one single day. Jenni reminds me to keep the door open for everyone at home, and Jenni reminds me to treat others, and myself, with deliberate kindness, because she does.

Kylea, sister-in-law and one of our "Helping Hands"

Jenni stood out as a beacon of light long before her diagnosis. I remember the very first time Jeff introduced us at some dive bar. I was so enamored by Jenni—and her light shone so bright—that I teased Jeff that even if their budding courtship didn't last, I hoped we could keep her as a friend. In just one meeting, she'd stolen my heart.

Fortunately for me, Jeff and Jenni's lovely relationship morphed into a most beautiful marriage, and I gained not just a friend, but a sister. Among all of the amazing qualities about Jenni (and they are countless), perhaps the singularly most remarkable to me is that I have never (not once!), ever heard Jenni complain about the cards she's been dealt.

In fact, I've heard people complain more in one conversation about the weather than I have ever heard Jenni utter about ALS in the past 7 1/2 years. The fact that she embraces life each day—and each moment—with not even an iota of bitterness, or expression of unfairness, seems superhuman. Jenni's inner steel and ability to take a bitter situation and shape it into a beautiful life existence— filled with love, community, and light—illustrate what an astounding spiritual alchemist she is. And if that's not worth learning from, I don't know what is.

Thank you, Jenni, for being such a profoundly inspirational teacher.

≈≈≈≈≈≈≈≈≈≈≈≈≈≈≈≈≈≈≈≈

Anne M., friend and one of our "Helping Hands"

Jenni has inspired and continues to inspire in so many ways. Her intellect is so vibrant and in combination with her graciousness, acute powers of observation, active listening, and a wicked sense of humor, teaches us all about living more fully. Her qualities of observation also help her to best use the talents of her many helpers who are eager to be the stand-in for Jenni's hands and feet, from household tasks to helping to bring her ideas to reality. I'm also learning how to pick my battles about priorities because of my time spent with Jenni. When I'm tempted to obsess about something ridiculous such as how something is folded or how the dishwasher is loaded, I remember that no matter the process, they'll be clean in the end!

Thank you, Jenni, Jeff, and Philip, for allowing me to be a part of your lives.

❧❧❧❧❧❧❧❧❧❧❧❧❧❧❧❧❧❧❧

Sharna M., Jeff's childhood friend

I first met Jenni during their wedding in Portland. I was very nervous to meet her. I had known Jeff since preschool, his was the very first number I memorized and we went to college together. We were each other's stand-by platonic date if we couldn't find someone else to go to a dance with.

What struck me most about Jenni was her beauty. I know she has many other great qualities, intelligence, and humor among them. However, she was radiant and stunning that weekend, not only on the day of her wedding, but every second I saw her.

When I first saw Jeff that weekend I noticed a huge change in him. Jeff always had a goofy laugh and sense of humor. But that weekend his smile was so bright, his face filled with so much light, and his eyes were colored with the kind of love so few people find in this lifetime.

I know how devoted Jeff has been to Jenni, but the reason is actually Jenni herself. Jenni has brought out the best in Jeff and I think he in her. They are a very lucky couple.

❧❧❧❧❧❧❧❧❧❧❧❧❧❧❧❧❧❧❧

Kathi C., friend and one of our "Helping Hands"

Jenni taught me to drink the watermelon juice, rather than pour it off the fruit. It is after all the best part.

She taught me it is not about completing the tasks, it is about enjoying conversation and including others, while doing what there is to do.

She invites me to be her hands while folding clothes and washing dishes. It seemed so simple a request. But it takes being present in the moment, with her, to actually be her completing the tasks with my hands. Channeling her love and energy into the clothes and dishes.

She sees the best in me and brings it forth in service. There is no more powerful request than that of another human being. Nor more stronger faith in another, that they will give you their best.

She approaches life from now on with "What's Next?" inviting her forward.

Being in her presence slows my mind to a quiet rumble and awakens my heart to love and grace and mercy and relationship and connection and life.

That is enough in all the best of ways.

❦❧❦❧❦❧❦❧❦❧❦❧❦❧❦❧❦❧❦❧❦❧❧

Kate S., medical school friend

Jenni is one of the most inspiring women that I know. She has always embraced life fully, and lights up every room she enters. She has a gift of being able to bring people together, and remember the sweetness in life. I was lucky enough to be study partners with Jenni through medical school. When I think back to our long hours of studying, my memories are of us laughing and finding enjoyment, even during the most stressful of times. When I find myself in challenging situations, I am reminded of my times with Jenni and her ability to find joy in even the most difficult times. This helps me to find it, too, and for this, I am forever grateful. I love you Jenni!

Suzi W., friend and one of our "Helping Hands"

Oh what an honor it is to be part of Jenni's full life . . .

When I am serving as a helper for her, I have had my doubts at times about my abilities to remember stuff in the process and hope I appear efficient. She keeps the humor side open and she helps me to forgive myself for mistakes.

I am continually in awe of her attitude, her patience, her spunk, her honesty, and courage during this challenging journey.

She teaches me these qualities by example. She greets her setbacks with a humble smile.

How could one not be affected positively by her ways??

She also teaches us not to be at the effect of mainstream medicine and makes choices on her own terms. Another vote for natural medicine and self-care. It is no wonder she has defied the odds and is a living proof of what is possible when dealt a "sucky hand."

I so admire that she also acknowledges the struggle that is hers but not like a victim. Another strong reminder that these two are mutually exclusive. I soak up her teachings regularly.

Many laughs and warm-hearted experiences occur when being out in public with Jenni. She is a rock star known by the community at Whole Foods and Trader Joe's to name a few. She is so willing to interact on a personal level with strangers who want to know her. It is enriching to observe how her sparkle affects others and me.

I first said yes to being on Jenni's team because my dear mother endured this same disease, and I wanted to know more of the process with someone outside my family and who took such a vital and proactive approach.

Jenni is my hero who personally helps me to put my "small stuff" in perspective. I see Jenni as a stellar example of accepting the things she cannot change and gently passing this on to others.

∽↭∾↭∾↭∾↭∾↭∾↭∾↭∾↭∾↭∾↭∾↭∾↭∾↭∾↭∾↭

Jessica A., college friend

Jenni and I were college freshman in 1994 when we met. We became close, loving, lifetime friends. She was an energetic, enthusiastic, positive, curious young woman back then, who embraced all that life had to offer. She embodies these very same qualities today, in spite of her illness. Jenni inspires me to be a loving supportive friend and to be the best person I can be. Her zest for new experiences, her appreciation for all the simple things, her sense of humor, her love of family and friends, make me want to be with her. Jenni has taught me to cherish those dear to me and to seize each day and make it a meaningful and worthwhile adventure.

∽↭∾↭∾↭∾↭∾↭∾↭∾↭∾↭∾↭∾↭∾↭∾↭∾↭∾↭∾↭

Rob and Gerri, brother and sister-in-law

Jenni is brave, passionate, and loving. When faced with ALS, she made a choice to accept a reality that would crush most of us. She didn't just merely accept ALS, she told it to FUCK OFF and thrived in it. Focusing on the present and not letting her physical limitations restrict her, she sought out life adventures and stretched the realm of what's possible. Focusing on living with a positive, people-focused attitude, she warmed the hearts and souls of those around her. Jenni is human and the struggle to accept ALS is real. But her courage to "walk the talk" and live in the face of her immense challenge is inspirational.

∽↭∾↭∾↭∾↭∾↭∾↭∾↭∾↭∾↭∾↭∾↭∾↭∾↭∾↭∾↭

Lindsay Y., childhood friend and one of our "Helping Hands"

Although Jenni may not know, I have learned valuable life lessons from her. I have learned that life isn't fair and sometimes when I want desperately to control an outcome, I have to come to accept that not everything is always in my control. I have learned that my attitude and my outlook on difficult situations is all I have and I cannot rely on others to find my inner strength. I have learned that each day is a precious gift and to be thankful for the beauty all around me. I have learned that it's ok to ask for help and to trust the people you love because we all need helping hands during certain challenges and tough times.

Jenni has also been an amazing teacher for my children. They know she is a mother, a wife, a daughter, and a friend, just like me. They have grown up accepting and understanding that we are the same yet different. They can see how we come together in a truly unique community to support each other, celebrate the good times, and lean on each other in the not so good times.

Life is unpredictable and will throw us curve balls when we are least expecting it, but Jenni has inspired me to be as positive as can be and to persevere. Her strength and courage is phenomenal and I am so lucky to have Jenni as my dear friend.

Lyn O., Landmark Seminar Leader and friend

Jenni is an amazing woman, but then, the apple doesn't fall from the tree.

Why does Jenni inspire me? I think because she doesn't pretend to be a saint. She's a very real person. I don't see her often, but the few times I have, I've been struck by her authenticity. She spoke at an event her mother gave, and she didn't drop drama about her voice sounding funny. Don't remember what she said, exactly, but whatever it was, it kept attention on the subject at hand while including her speech hesitation but without heroics. Then I went to a party she was giving—it was an opportunity for her to let loved ones and friends see and enjoy her, ask questions, spend time with her and enjoy a lovely dinner. She was natural, she wasn't keeping up a front—she was honest about her fears and her disappointment, about sometimes feeling sorry for herself, and what she was grateful for.

Jenni inspires me because she's still herself, normal and natural. She doesn't demand or want sympathy but she's not a martyr. Around her, empathy goes both ways. She is one of us, human, going through something that few people have to experience, but allowing it to serve as a genuine connection between human beings. Jenni inspires me because she continues to do the best she can with what she has to work with, making her one extraordinary lady.

"Hope is being able to see that there is light despite all of the darkness" ~ Desmond Tutu

᠅᠅᠅᠅᠅᠅᠅᠅᠅᠅᠅᠅᠅᠅᠅᠅᠅᠅᠅᠅

Mickie G., family friend (hosted my baby shower) and one of our "Helping Hands"

As an occupational therapist, I marvel at Jenni's creativity and problem-solving skills. She always does what she can to be as independent as possible. She is always gracious and thankful to her caregivers and friends, even if we say something insensitive or do the wrong thing! She stays engaged in her family's lives and in the community and tries to give back whenever possible. I can truly say she lives life to the fullest.

Now a word about her family; her mother Joyce and her husband Jeff are always mastering the difficult task of juggling being caregivers but remaining family first. They appear to respect Jenni's decisions and personal space even though she cannot always implement her wishes without their assistance. They have also managed to amass a considerable support system of extended families and friends who willingly aid with transportation and day-to-day tasks. This is a testimony to their grace and positive outlook.

Tammy L., friend and one of our "Helping Hands"

Jenni is inspiration. She is the rock . . . the heart of a village that I'm so grateful to be a part of. I truly enjoy spending time with her. I just love her humor, her patience, and the quiet strength she exudes. Behind her beautiful smile I see the most beautiful soul. Thank you for leaving your sparkle wherever you go!

Amy B., medical school mentor and friend

Jenni is the epitome of beauty, resilience, and strength. She is SUCH an inspiration to me, my daughter, and so many others. I love this woman with all my heart!

Steve, brother-in-law

What Jenni means to me is more than I can express in words. She has my upmost respect and admiration. She is kind, caring and gentle, yet principled and fierce. That is a combination of characteristics I have rarely found in one person. Frankly, she is who I want to be when I grow up. That is what I love about Jenni.

Victoria C., friend and one of our "Helping Hands"

The start of one of the prayers that we say before the Sh'ma reads, "Open up our eyes. Teach us how to live. Fill our hearts with joy and all the love you have to give." I am inspired by Jenni in many ways, but chiefly because every day she chooses to live with ALS instead of to die while she is living with ALS. She does this despite the crushing inevitable truth of her situation. Jenni allows each of us in to know her as she truly is. We get to help her have her fullest expression of herself when we do for her what she physically can't do for herself.

Jenni receives this with grace and this enriches the experience of each of us who are part of her circle. I am always moved by her and how it feels to be with her. Her everyday grace inspires me to dig deep to re-examine my choices and recognize my blessings. Her presence in my life is a blessing.

Natasha K., medical school friend

Being with Jenni is infectious delight. Maya Angelou once said that "I've learned that people will forget what you said, people will forget what you did, but people will never forget how you made them feel." Certainly when I think about Jenni, I recall her funny and heartfelt stories, our precious and joyous memories together but most of all, I think about how she has and continues to make me feel. With her radiantly beautiful eyes, her deliciously sweet (sometimes mischievous) smile, she looks at you showering unconditional love without doing or saying a word. She has a unique generosity, a giving of unconditional affection and acceptance, and an ability to see the best self in the people around her.

Having her in my life inspires me to be more forgiving, more accepting and more loving of others. And how she has handled her diagnosis, the fading away of her physical body, has inspired me to be more grateful for what I have but has also inspired me to BE a better human being. To shine the best parts of my spirit outward, as Jenni does. Others will glean the benefit of my patience, warmth, and love as a result of what I have learned from Jenni just being Jenni. Our relationship is one of my heart's greatest treasures.

❦❧❦❧❦❧❦❧❦❧❦❧❦❧❦❧❦❧❦❧❦❧❦❧

Lindsey M., Jeff's childhood friend and one of our "Helping Hands"

Jenni is light. And warmth. A true friend.

She is the best smile.

Jenni is knowing. And empathy. A humble teacher.

She is a gift in the truest sense of the word.

Jenni brings people together. People who love her, now love each other.

She is a blessing waiting to land on your shoulder. An inspiration you didn't know you needed.

Jenni will always will be all of these things, and more. Forever. Words can't express my gratitude for knowing you Jenni.

❦❧❦❧❦❧❦❧❦❧❦❧❦❧❦❧❦❧❦❧❦❧❦❧

Sharon M., friend & seamstress

My first meeting with Jenni was a little like love at first sight.... I immediately felt Jenni's deep calm, centered spirit. I am honored to sew for her, each stitch a worship of our mutual divine!

Jenni Berebitsky's Fan Club

Lisa, a.k.a "our cruise director," spearheaded this delightful group of Jenni's friends and family. Their mission, which they chose to accept, was and continues to be creating unique ways for getting together, deepening their bond of sisterhood, & expanding their intellect, while always having lots of fun.

38th B-Day Party
(5 years after diagnosis)

Jenni's Birthday Parties

41st B-Day Party
(8 years after
diagnosis)

42nd B-Day
Party
(8 years,
11 months
after diagnosis)

Jenni Berebitsky's Fan Club

**T
H
E
A
T
E
R**

Dirty Dancing
Clowes Memorial Hall
(6 years, 3 months after diagnosis)

Hamilton, Chicago, IL
(7 years, 7 months
after diagnosis)

Flashdance
Clowes Memorial Hall
(4 years, 7 months after diagnosis)

Wanda Sykes

Murat Theatre, Old National Centre (7 years, 6 months after diagnosis)

Taping of NPR's show
Wait, Wait, Don't Tell Me
(6 years, 6 months after diagnosis)

Beautiful: the Carole King Musical
Clowes Memorial Hall
(9 years, 11 months after diagnosis)

Jenni Berebitsky's Fan Club

Matisse: Life in Color
Indianapolis Museum
of Art (IMA)
(4 years, 9 months
after diagnosis)

*Georgia O'Keeffe
and the Southwestern
Still Life*, IMA
(5 years, 10 months
after diagnosis)

*First Look: Contemporary
Design Galleries*, IMA
(8 years, 5 months
after diagnosis)

You don't need your eyes examined. Our photo was pointillized with an iPad app and we became a Neo-Impressionist style painting.

Face to Face: The Neo-Impressionist Portrait, IMA
(5 years, 5 months
after diagnosis)

Dogs: Faithful and True,
Eiteljorg Museum
(8 years, 1 month
after diagnosis)

Winterlights at Newfields (IMA)
(8 years, 9 months after diagnosis)

Gallery talk: *Closer Look:
Sights and Sounds,* IMA
(8 years, 8 months
after diagnosis)

Jenni Berebitsky's Fan Club

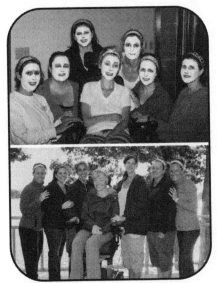

Heartland Film opening night of
The Fault in Our Stars
(5 years, 3 months
after diagnosis)

Ladies' Lake Retreat on
Sylvan Lake, Rome City, IN
(3 years, 6 months
after diagnosis)

Opening night of Heartland
Film Festival 2016
(7 years, 7 months
after diagnosis)

Pool Party at Barb & Charlie's
(7 years, 6 months after diagnosis)

John & Hank Green Tour
promoting John's new novel
Indianapolis, IN
(8 years, 7 months after diagnosis)

Jenni Berebitsky's Fan Club

White Elephant Parties

Jenni could not stop blinking from the flash, so on the 12th try Lisa gave up and had everyone close their eyes. (4 years, 9 months after diagnosis)

(7 years, 1 month after diagnosis)

(8 years, 9 months after diagnosis)

Jenni Berebitsky's Fan Club

Indianapolis Hebrew Congregation Women's Passover Seders

2014
(5 years
after diagnosis)

2015
(6 years
after diagnosis)

2016
(7 years,
1 month
after diagnosis)

2017
(8 years
after diagnosis)

About the Author

Jenni, 7 years, 9 months after diagnosis

Jenni Berebitsky was diagnosed with ALS (Lou Gehrig's disease) in March 2009. She has been living through the ups and downs of this relentless disease with her family and friends by her side every step of the way.

Jenni earned her BA in psychology from Beloit College in 1998 and her naturopathic medical degree from the National College of Natural Medicine in Portland, Oregon, in 2007. She resides in Indianapolis, Indiana, with her loving husband, Jeff, and their vibrant son, Philip.

Jenni relishes the memories of past adventures: moving to the Pacific Northwest after college; studying abroad in Melbourne, Australia; backpacking through Southeast Asia; traveling to Tuscany to partake in the olive harvest; and sea kayaking alongside orca whales.

Currently, she enjoys laughing and growing with her husband; guiding her passionate son as he takes on life; spending countless hours with her mom writing this book; dispensing her knowledge of naturopathic medicine with wannabe patients; visiting the Indianapolis Museum of Art and other activities with friends and family; listening to audio books; keeping up with her favorite TV shows and movies; and being a member of the jury for the Heartland Film's Truly Moving Picture Award.

Jenni looks to the future with excitement and anticipation of new adventures, including the release of a documentary about her life, *30 Minutes*.

Made in the USA
Lexington, KY
21 March 2018